NAVIGATING THE FUTURE WITH SCENARIO PLANNING: A Guidebook for Librarians

Joan Giesecke
Jon Cawthorne
Deb Pearson

Association of College and Research Libraries
A division of the American Library Association
Chicago, Illinois 2015

The paper used in this publication meets the minimum requirements of American National Standard for Information Sciences–Permanence of Paper for Printed Library Materials, ANSI Z39.48-1992. ∞

Library of Congress Cataloging-in-Publication Data

Giesecke, Joan.
  Navigating the future with scenario planning : a guidebook for librarians / by Joan Giesecke, Jon Cawthorne, Deb Pearson.
     pages cm
  Includes bibliographical references and index.
  ISBN 978-0-8389-8751-3 (pbk. : alk. paper) -- ISBN 978-0-8389-8752-0 (pdf) -- ISBN 978-0-8389-8753-7 (epub) -- ISBN 978-0-8389-8754-4 (kindle) 1. Library planning. 2. Academic libraries--United States--Planning--Case studies. 3. Organizational change. I. Cawthorne, Jon E. II. Pearson, Debra. III. Title.
  Z678.G537 2015
  025.1'977--dc23
                        2015018855

Printed in the United States of America.
19 18 17 16 15 5 4 3 2 1

TABLE OF CONTENTS

PART I [THE SCENARIO PLANNING PROCESS]

Chapter 1. Introduction **1**

Joan Giesecke and Jon Cawthorne

A Theory of Scenario Planning 2
Scenario Planning versus Strategic Planning 4
A History of Scenario Planning 5
Scenarios and Scenario Planning 7
Navigating the Book 7
Notes 8

Chapter 2. Scenario Planning Theories **11**

Joan Giesecke and Deb Pearson

Scenario Planning Models 11
Schwartz
Schoemaker
Ralston and Wilson
Lindgren and Bandhold
Wade
Mercer
Chermack
Designing the Scenario Planning Process 15
Organizational Readiness
Identifying the Focal Issue or Question
Identifying the Steps in the
Scenario Planning Process 16
Choosing the Scenario Planning Team 16
Beginning Scenario Planning 17
Ranking the Forces and Choosing the Driving Forces .. 18
Developing the Scenarios 19
Determining the Implications of the Scenarios 19
A Brief Example of Scenario Development 20
Conclusion 24
Notes 25

Chapter 3. Writing Scenario Plots **27**

Joan Giesecke and Deb Pearson

Scenario Styles 28
Major Plot Lines 31
Winners and Losers
Challenge and Response
Evolution

Other Plot Ideas.. 31
Revolution
Cycles
Infinite Possibilities
Lone Ranger
Writing the Story.. 33
Conclusion 35
Notes.. 35

Chapter 4. Developing Strategies for Scenarios 37
Joan Giesecke and Deb Pearson

Developing Strategies...................................... 37
Displaying Strategies....................................... 39
Conclusion 40
Notes.. 43

PART 2 [ESSAYS AND CASE STUDIES]

**Chapter 5. Using Complementary Research Methods
to Enhance Scenario Planning 47**
Tyler Walters

Introduction.. 47
Scenario Planning versus Using Scenarios 49
Research Methods... 49
Delphi Method
Semi-structured Interview Method
Case Study Method
*Semi-structured Interview Method
   in Case Study Construction*
Stratified and Purposive Sampling
Conclusion 55
Notes.. 55

Chapter 6. Scenarios on Higher Education 57
Tyler Walters

International Higher Education Scenarios
   and Research Programs 57
International Scenario Drivers........................... 59
North American Scenario Studies
   of Higher Education 61
International Scenario Studies of University
   Research Trends 62
University Library–Related Scenario Studies............. 65
Tips for Using Higher Education Scenarios.............. 67
Notes.. 68

**Chapter 7. How Scenarios Help Organizational Leaders
Think Creatively about Change** 73
Jon Cawthorne

    Defining Culture and Development of Groups 74
    Leadership for Change 77
    Conclusion 79
    Notes 79

**Chapter 8. Scenarios for Planning with
Human Resource Directors** 81
Jon Cawthorne

    The Importance of Human Resource Directors 82
    Four Scenarios 83
    The Case Study Institutions and Choice of Scenarios .. 91
    Human Resource Directors in the Four Case Studies ... 92
        Case A
        Case B
        Case C
        Case D
    Responses by the Human Resources Directors 94
        Similarities across All Case Study Sites
        Differences across Case Study Sites
    Conclusion 99
    Notes 101

**Chapter 9. University of Nebraska–Lincoln Student
Technology Fee Case Study Updated** 103
Joan Giesecke and Deb Pearson

    Student Technology Fee: A Case Study
        at the University of Nebraska–Lincoln 104
        Background
        Process
        Identifying the Drivers for Change
        Linking the Key Factors
        Producing the Initial Mini-scenario Elements
        Reducing the Number of Scenarios to Two
        Writing the Scenarios
        Identifying Issues That Arise
    The Case Study Revisited 108
    Lessons Learned 109
    Conclusion 112
    Notes 112

Bibliography 113

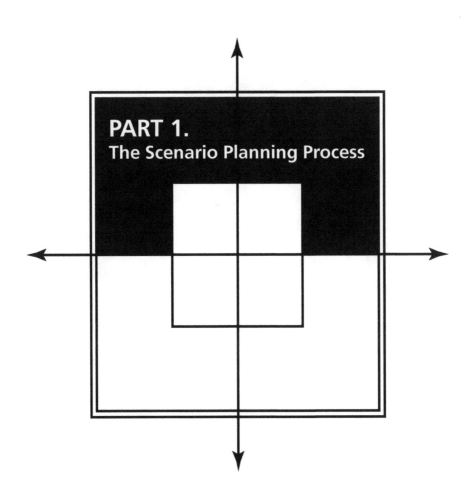

PART 1.
The Scenario Planning Process

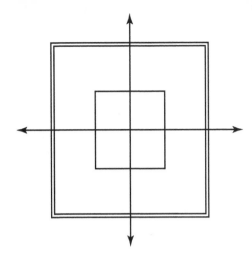

CHAPTER 1

INTRODUCTION

Joan Giesecke and Jon Cawthorne

LIBRARY LEADERS EXIST in an environment of constant organizational shifting and settling, with change occurring at an increasing rate. Changes in technology, social structure, and government policies, to name just a few areas, challenge today's leaders to anticipate how the future might develop and to craft strategies that will help their organizations cope in uncertain environments. Leaders have tried any number of planning systems to be successful, including strategic planning, long-range planning, short-range planning, reengineering, redesigning, and reframing organizations.

Traditional planning systems, such as those noted above, focus on an organization's opportunities for incremental change. The strategic directions developed in the planning process become the road maps for organizational action. Managers concentrate on executing the plans to achieve agreed-to goals, all the while not acknowledging that the environment is in constant flux.

Managers using a road map paradigm believe that
- ultimate objectives are known, perhaps because someone has achieved them before
- the terrain is stable
- detours are generally well-marked
- the rules of the road do not change
- the world responds slowly to change[1]

1

Today's leaders need a different paradigm to guide their planning processes. In an uncertain environment, the metaphor of a fighter pilot who uses radar to chart a course provides an approach that can help leaders respond to change. Pilots need to anticipate problems, avoid hazards, and make adjustments as conditions change. Leaders who view the world from the perspective of a pilot believe that

- objectives are evolving and uncertain
- organizations must keep moving or they will crash
- threats and opportunities are constantly changing
- there is no fixed frame of reference
- there are no rules[2]

Leaders need tools, then, that will help them anticipate change and create strategies that will be effective in uncertain times. For these leaders, scenarios and scenario planning techniques provide a guide for developing visions, goals, objectives, and strategies that can help managers and their staff throughout organizations thrive in uncertain times.

In scenario-driven planning, leaders work together to develop plausible scenarios, or stories about possible futures. Using these stories, organizations can then design strategies that will help move the organization forward. Scenario-driven planning helps managers identify assumptions about the future and the organization and use that information to review and renew the organization.[3] It is a disciplined planning methodology for imagining multiple possible futures in which organizational decision making can be played out.[4]

In contrast to imagining possible futures, some futurists concentrate on probable futures, which are scenarios developed by extrapolating from the present to the future, examining demographic trends, and using history to explain what might happen in the future. Other futurists work on preferable futures, where the organization develops an image or vision of what it hopes the future will entail and then uses that vision to guide organizational actions. Scenario planning, on the other hand, includes identifying multiple futures or scenarios to encourage decision makers to look for discontinuities in today's events and to speculate about possible changes in the environment that could have an impact on the organization.[5]

A Theory of Scenario Planning
When defining scenario planning, some have suggested it is more art than science, and while it should remain an art, scenario planning needs to be

grounded in theory and science. In 2003, while many scholars were researching this area, Thomas Chermack introduced a theory of scenario planning and—describes six domains that are the building blocks of scenario planning theory.

1. *Dialogue, conversation quality, and engagement:* Dialogue is the first step in scenario planning and allows an organization and the individuals that make up the organization to expand their collective thinking. Through dialogue, conversation and engagement, experiences, knowledge, and assumptions are shared throughout the planning project. They allow people to experiment with ideas by taking facts and data and applying them in imagined and speculative futures. Effective conversation or conversation quality is fundamental to sharing mental models that help all members engage with the organization and gain a common understanding of the organization and the external environment.[6]

2. *Learning:* Because learning is essential to any good scenario planning process, some experts have described planning as essentially a learning activity. Chermack defined learning as "the process of gaining knowledge or skill."[7] In scenario planning, learning is the process of understanding the internal and external environments and how these environments interact. Learning takes place during the analysis of trends and driving forces that will impact the future of the organization, during the identification of strategies, and during the making of decisions about how to proceed as an organization.

3. *Mental models:* Mental models are internal constructs that embody how individuals see and know the world. They are based on the assumptions individuals make about how the world works. As the environment changes, individuals adjust their internal mental models to incorporate these changes into their thinking. In scenario planning, group and individual learning takes place when often long-held assumptions or mental models are questioned. Introducing new mental models allows re-examination of these assumptions and opens the possibility for learning.

4. *Decision making:* Decision making for both the organization and the individuals comes out of the first three domains. Scenario planning promotes flexibility in decision making by allowing in-

dividuals to consider alternative futures in developing strategies and to revise decisions as the future develops. Scenarios help leaders develop a process that will ultimately improve decision making.[8] Peter Schwartz, president and founder of the Global Business network, stated that developing scenarios starts by looking inward at conscious or unconscious mind-sets to make judgments about the future.[9] Scenarios ask people to suspend their disbelief long enough to appreciate the impact of the scenario. A scenario is effective when someone pondering an issue that was taboo or unthinkable in the past says, "Yes. I can see how that might happen—and what I might do as a result."[10]

5. *Leadership:* Just as decisions are one outcome of scenario planning, leadership development is also an outcome of the process. Chermack included a summary of research studies linking leadership development and scenario planning, demonstrating that planning skills are becoming crucial for today's leaders.[11]

6. *Organizational performance and change:* In scenario planning theory, all previous domains, used together, combine to improve organizational performance and guide change. Chermack noted the need for additional research to demonstrate the connection between successful scenario planning processes and improvements in individual and organizational performance.[12]

As stated above, these six domains of scenario planning theory are the building blocks an organization uses to begin a planning process. Scenario planning is unique in that it brings together these domains in a way that facilitates organizational change.[13]

Scenario Planning versus Strategic Planning

Scenario planning, then, is a planning tool that is different from the "predict the future and work toward it" approach of traditional planning models. Schwartz believes that when leaders undertake strategic planning, denial acts as a valve that automatically shuts off creativity and alternative solutions.[14] Developing scenario thinking is an incremental step in strategic planning and advancing the leader's view of different possibilities.[15] Scenario thinking, therefore, can become a useful part of strategic planning. Scenario planning does not focus on accurately predicting the future.

Rather, the process describes a number of possible futures that are credible and yet uncertain. The descriptions of possible futures are then used to develop organizational strategies.[16] In contrast, strategic planning assumes that the future is an extension of past trends. It relies on quantitative, statistical models to help managers design plans to meet agreed-to goals and objectives. It assumes a level of certainty in the environment to guide planning. Scenario planning includes more variables in planning and treats the future not as simple and certain, but as uncertain and capable of developing in multiple ways. It also allows organizations to actively create the future instead of waiting passively for one to arrive. The purpose of planning is to develop policies and decisions to guide the actions of individuals in the organization. Scenario planning is particularly effective not only for exploring a variety of future outcomes, but also for surfacing greater awareness of parts of the organization that are not seen, such as an organization's culture. The real value of scenario planning is the way it engages participants in having conversations that lead to learning, changing mental models, making decisions, and reconsidering long-held assumptions, all of which lead to organizational change.[17]

A History of Scenario Planning

The use of "what if" narrative scenarios for organizational planning started with Herman Kahn and the RAND Corporation. After World War II, RAND used scenarios to research new forms of weapons technology. Kahn pioneered the technique of "future-now" thinking, which involved a detailed analysis plus the use of imagination to write a myth or story as if it were written by people living in the future.[18] Kahn's scenarios helped people break past their mental blocks and consider "unthinkable" futures. Early on, Kahn's founding of the Hudson Institute earned him the title of America's top futurist. By the late 1950s, many companies and organizations used scenarios. The work of the Hudson Institute brought the scenario process to corporations such as Corning, IBM, and General Motors.

In 1947, Stanford University established the Stanford Research Institute (SRI) to offer long-range planning for business, incorporating operations research, economics, and political strategy alongside science and military consulting.[19]

The SRI "futures group" began to ask questions and apply scenario thinking to a variety of disciplines to study the future. These questions did not focus only on military and weaponry science; they led to predictions of "large-scale educational teaching machine systems" by 1973; "low-cost 3D colour television" by 1977; "undersea motels, factories, and recreation centres powered by nuclear power"; and "commercial passenger rockets going to the moon by 1980."[20] While top scientists in other companies asked, "What will the world want and need in the next twenty years?" SRI focused on straight-line numeric forecasts and gathered literature on utopias and dystopias from science fiction to create plausible scenarios.[21]

A great advancement in scenarios and future thinking occurred at Royal Dutch Shell. Pierre Wack and Ted Newland developed scenario thinking at Shell in the early 1970s, a critical time in the oil industry with the emergence of a consortium of petroleum exporting countries. Wack and Newland had written two future scenarios: one presented the conventional wisdom that oil prices would stay stable; the second outlined a more plausible future—an oil price crisis sparked by the actions of the Organization of Petroleum Exporting Countries (OPEC). Although the managers received, read, and understood the implications of the scenarios, little changed in organizational decision making. The breakthrough came when Wack and Newland realized that the scenarios, or stories, needed to change management's view of reality. They revised the scenarios to show the full implications of a major increase in oil prices. The purpose of the scenarios was to help managers and people at all levels change their view of reality—to match it up more closely with reality as it is, and reality as it was going to be.[22] With this changed view of reality, Royal Dutch Shell developed a variety of strategies to use in case of a major change in oil prices and therefore navigated the significant oil price crisis brought on by OPEC in 1973. Shell was able to address a broad range of strategic and planning decisions across the uncertainties of time and politics.[23] By the late 1970s, most Fortune 100 corporations were using some form of scenario planning to help them cope with the uncertainty of the times.[24]

With the recession and economic challenges of the 1980s, corporations decreased staffing in their planning departments, and the use of scenario planning declined. By the beginning of the twenty-first century, corporations again turned to scenario planning techniques to help them develop strategies for coping with uncertainty and ambiguity in the environment. Scenario planning has not been used only by corporations. It has also been used in a wide variety of settings, from national governments and corporations looking at change opportunities, to higher education associations, universities, and libraries. It is used in conjunction with visioning efforts and strategic planning as part of a comprehensive organizational planning process.

Scenarios and Scenario Planning

The terms *scenario planning* and *using scenarios in planning* are often used interchangeably, although they describe different processes. Scenario planning, as described above, is a structured planning methodology for developing multiple stories about plausible futures for organizations to use in developing strategies and addressing issues of an uncertain future. In contrast, organizations may choose to use scenarios developed by others to promote creative thinking in the planning process. Scenarios take complex elements and weave them into a coherent story to challenge current thinking and promote reconsideration of mental models. Scenarios help leaders take into account the complexities of the current environment and consider the implications of these complexities for the future of the organization. Scenarios may be used as a tool in strategic planning efforts to help the organization consider the need to change in order to thrive under conditions of uncertainty. However, using scenarios created outside of the organization limits organizational learning and leadership development, which are by-products of the process of creating scenarios. Therefore, in choosing a planning process, leaders need to consider not only the planning tools they wish to use, but also the organizational outcomes that are part of the chosen planning method.

Navigating the Book

This guidebook updates the 1998 book *Scenario Planning for Libraries* and provides today's leaders with information on how to use this powerful planning tool in addressing concerns about the future of libraries in times of increasing change.[25]

Part I of this guidebook, which includes chapter 1–4, describes the basic technique for conducting a scenario planning process. This section provides the reader with step-by-step instructions on how to carry out scenario planning. Chapter 2 describes various approaches that can be used in conducting scenario planning efforts. Details are provided on each of the steps in the scenario planning process. Chapter 3 provides tips on writing the scenarios, or stories, in a way that will engage decision makers in thinking creatively about the future. Chapter 4 provides ideas on how to develop strategies from scenarios. By the end of part I, the reader has the tools needed to facilitate scenario planning activities.

Part II includes a series of essays on how scenarios and scenario planning can be used to help organizations address uncertainty in the environment. Each essay explores different ways in which organizations can introduce change into their structures. In chapters 5 and 6, Tyler Walters identifies how scenarios can be used with other planning techniques to help organizations thrive in an uncertain future and discusses scenarios used in higher education. Chapter 7 describes how organizational leaders can use scenarios to implement organizational change and address issues of organizational culture. Part II also includes two case studies of libraries using scenarios and scenario planning in their organizations to address important yet uncertain issues. In chapter 8, Jon Cawthorne relates his research on the role of human resource directors in addressing issues of organizational change. Chapter 9 provides an update on how the University of Nebraska–Lincoln successfully used scenario planning to determine how to best implement a student technology fee. The chapter outlines how the university has used this process for the past fifteen years to work with students on the use of the technology fee.

Notes

1. Joan Giesecke, *Scenario Planning for Libraries* (Chicago: American Library Association, 1998), 19.
2. Ibid.
3. Ibid., viii.
4. Paul J. H. Schoemaker, "Scenario Planning: A Tool for Strategic Thinking," *MIT Sloan Management Review* 36, no. 2 (Winter 1995): 25.
5. Giesecke, *Scenario Planning for Libraries*, 4–5.
6. Thomas J. Chermack, *Scenario Planning in Organizations: How to Create, Use, and Access Scenarios* (San Francisco: Berrett-Koehler, 2011), 32–33.
7. Ibid., 35.
8. Thomas J. Chermack, "A Methodology for Assessing Performance-Based Scenario Planning," *Journal of Leadership and Organizational Studies* 10, no. 2 (Fall 2003): 55–63. doi:10.1177/107179190301000206.
9. Peter Schwartz, *The Art of the Long View: Planning for the Future in an Uncertain World* (New York: Doubleday, 1991): 59.

10. Ibid., 39.
11. Chermack, *Scenario Planning in Organizations*, 53.
12. Ibid., 56.
13. Ibid., 58.
14. Schwartz, *Art of the Long View*, 11.
15. Richard A. Swanson, "Seeing Scenarios," *Advances in Developing Human Resources* 10, no. 2 (May 2008): 127–28, doi:10.1177/1523422307313335.
16. Shawn M. Keough and Kevin J. Shanahan, "Scenario Planning: Toward a More Complete Model for Practice," *Advances in Developing Human Resources* 10, no. 2 (May 2008): 167, doi:10.1177/1523422307313311.
17. Jon Edward Cawthorne, "Viewing the Future of University Research Libraries through the Perspectives of Scenarios" (PhD diss., Simmons, 2013), 2–3.
18. Gill Ringland, *Scenario Planning: Managing for the Future*, 2nd ed. (Winchester, NY: Wiley and Sons, 2006).
19. Mats Lindgren and Hans Bandhold, *Scenario Planning: The Link between Future and Strategy* (New York: Palgrave Macmillan, 2009), 37
20. Ibid., 14.
21. Ibid., 15.
22. Schwartz, *Art of the Long View*.
23. Cawthorne, "Viewing the Future," 18.
24. Chermack, *Scenario Planning in Organizations*, 12.
25. Giesecke, *Scenario Planning for Libraries*.

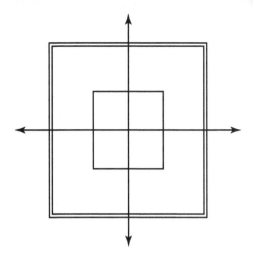

CHAPTER 2

SCENARIO PLANNING THEORIES

Joan Giesecke and Deb Pearson

Scenario Planning Models

A WIDE VARIETY of scenario planning models have emerged as researchers and planners develop processes to engage organizational decision makers in addressing questions about the future. Models present a varying number of steps in the process, from five steps for an abbreviated version to well over eighteen steps for a very detailed approach. This chapter presents a number of scenario planning models and describes the various steps.

Schwartz

One of the most frequently used models of scenario planning is the process developed by Peter Schwartz in his book *The Art of the Long View*. Schwartz detailed eight steps for the scenario planning process:

1. Identify the focal issue or decision.
2. Identify key factors in the local environment.
3. Identify the driving forces that influence the key factors.
4. Identify which forces are the most important and the most uncertain.
5. Select the most important force and the most uncertain force, to create the scenario matrix.

6. Complete the scenarios.
7. Consider the implications of each scenario.
8. Select leading indicators and signposts.[1]

Schoemaker

Paul Schoemaker developed a model for scenario planning that links scenarios with strategic thinking. He presented ten possible steps for decision makers to follow in developing scenarios to use in planning. The steps are designed to compensate for errors in decision making resulting from overconfidence in one's ability to predict the future and tunnel vision in thinking about the future:

1. Define the scope of the issue to be addressed, including time frame and scope of analysis.
2. Identify the major stakeholders to include in the planning process.
3. Identify basic trends in the environment.
4. Identify key uncertainties among the trends that will impact the issue under discussion.
5. Construct initial scenario themes, including both a positive and a negative view of the issue.
6. Check for consistency and plausibility among the scenario outlines.
7. Develop learning scenarios from the identified themes.
8. Identify research needs of the stakeholders to further understanding of uncertainties and trends.
9. Develop quantitative methods to assess the scenarios.
10. Evolve toward decision scenarios that can be used by decision makers to assess strategies.[2]

Ralston and Wilson

In *The Scenario Planning Handbook*, Bill Ralston and Ian Wilson presented a detailed, step-by-step approach to developing and using scenarios. Their process includes eighteen steps:

1. Develop the case for scenarios to be used in planning.
2. Gain the understanding, support, and participation of the ultimate decision makers..
3. Define the decision focus.

4. Design the process.
5. Select the facilitator.
6. Form the scenario planning team.
7. Gather available data, views, and projections.
8. Identify and assess key decision factors.
9. Identify the critical forces among the decision factors.
10. Conduct focused research on key issues and forces.
11. Assess the importance and predictability or uncertainty of forces.
12. Identify key "axes of uncertainty" for the structure of the scenarios.
13. Select the logic or basic outline of the scenarios.
14. Write the story lines.
15. Rehearse the future with scenarios.
16. Make decision recommendations.
17. Identify the signposts to monitor.
18. Communicate the results to the organization.[3]

Lindgren and Bandhold

Mats Lindgren and Hans Bandhold presented a different approach to scenario planning called TAIDA.[4] Once a focal question for the planning process is identified, the authors propose the following framework for scenario planning projects:

Tracking: Trace changes, threats, and opportunities in the environment.

Analyzing: Analyze changes in the environment and generate scenarios.

Imaging: Create images of what is desired from the plausible futures.

Deciding: Develop strategies to meet the threats and achieve the vision.

Acting: Take action and assess results.[5]

Wade

Woody Wade, in *Scenario Planning: A Field Guide to the Future*, presented a ten-step process, including six steps for creating scenarios and four steps for using the scenarios for decision making.

1. Frame the challenge or question to be addressed.
2. Gather information about the environment.

3. Identify the driving forces.
4. Define the future's critical uncertainties.
5. Generate the scenarios.
6. Create the story lines.
7. Validate the scenarios.
8. Assess the implications of the scenarios and possible responses.
9. Identify signposts.
10. Monitor and update the scenarios.[6]

Mercer

For organizations seeking a simpler approach to scenario planning, David Mercer provided a six-step process that can be used when an organization has a good grasp of the environmental factors and trends that impact the focal question for the planning process.[7]

1. Decide the drivers for change.
2. Bring the identified drivers together into a viable framework.
3. Produce initial mini-scenarios.
4. Reduce the number of mini-scenarios to two or three to develop further.
5. Write the scenarios.
6. Identify the issues arising from the scenarios.

Chermack

Thomas Chermack discussed the theoretical foundations for scenario planning and provided a performance-based system in his work *Scenario Planning for Organizations: How to Create, Use, and Assess Scenarios.* He grouped the planning activities into five major categories.

1. *Project preparation:* Define the scope of the project. Identify team members.
2. *Scenario exploration:* Identify environmental factors.
3. *Scenario development:* Rank forces by impact and uncertainty. Develop scenario logics or outline and write the stories.
4. *Scenario implementation:* Use scenarios to analyze current strategies and develop signals for assessing the accuracy of the stories.
5. *Project assessment:* Assess results of the planning process.[8]

Designing the Scenario Planning Process

Identifying factors in two key areas will help the organization decide if a scenario planning process will be effective for it. First is the organizational culture or organizational readiness to complete a scenario planning process. Second is the focal question that the organization wants to address.

Organizational Readiness

To decide if scenario planning will be a successful planning strategy, decision makers should review three internal factors that affect strategic decision making. First, an organizational culture that is highly participative and encourages thinking about the future will be more compatible with scenario planning than one that is more strictly hierarchical. In addition, the organization has to be open to input from and participation by a variety of stakeholders, including external stakeholders, in the process. Second, there has to be support from the top executives for the organization or unit to encourage participation in the scenario planning process. Resistance by the leadership of the organization will undermine the process. Because scenario planning is a fundamental change in how strategies are developed, senior leaders need to be open to a change in mind-set for scenario planning to be useful. Third, the organizational decision makers must be interested in and willing to look beyond short-term problems to long-term questions. The time frame for a scenario planning issue should be at least five years into the future but no more than fifteen years. This time frame will give decision makers time to make changes in the organization but is not so distant that the scenarios no longer seem realistic or plausible to the decision makers. Reviewing these internal factors will help decision makers determine when to use scenario planning in their strategic planning efforts.[9]

Identifying the Focal Issue or Question

The scenario planning process is designed around a question that centers on the uncertainty of the future and how the organization may respond to changes in the environment. The focus should be on issues that are important to the future success of the organization. These are the issues that keep leaders up at night. The focus can be as broad as looking at the future for a particular service or product to as narrow as looking at how a unit may be impacted by changes in the environment. Questions such as "What changes in technology will have an impact on our organization?" or "Should we begin a new service?" or "How will our customers change in relation to the changing demographics in the US?" would be well-served by scenario planning.

A question that is too narrow and specific may benefit from more traditional planning processes. Choosing a new technology system in a short time frame may be addressed by a standard purchasing process. On the other hand, examining major changes in how technology is used may be more appropriate for a scenario planning process, which treats the future as uncertain and trends as in flux.

Identifying the Steps in the Scenario Planning Process

As illustrated by the list of models above, a variety of approaches can be used in developing a scenario planning process for an organization. Organizations should choose a model that matches their organizational culture. For example, for organizations with a culture that supports planning and with internal facilitators who can manage the process, the standard model from Schwartz will likely work quite well.[10] It includes all of the core features of scenario planning: environmental analysis, identification of driving forces, development of a matrix of most uncertain and most important forces, completion of the scenarios, and development of strategies to guide future planning. For organizations that want to completely change their planning system or that do not have an established planning process, the work of Ralston and Wilson may be most useful.[11] It is the most detailed of the planning models and breaks down the steps into smaller segments.

Once an organization has identified the steps to use in the scenario planning process, it helps to review what should be accomplished in each step. The next sections summarize the activities that are part of each of the core steps in scenario planning.

Choosing the Scenario Planning Team

Once leaders have confirmed that scenario planning is an appropriate process to use to address a key strategic question facing the organization, they can begin to put together the scenario planning participants or team who will complete the process of creating scenarios. The team should include "key decision makers within the organization, employees at varying levels within the company [i.e. organization] with knowledge of each functional area, and professional or industry experts from outside the company [i.e. organization]."[12]

Team members should represent all major stakeholders, such as faculty, staff, students, and community members. Include people with different intellectual and cultural backgrounds, those that have a good knowledge of the organization and who will be willing to think beyond the short term to possible long-term changes that the organization may face. Team members also need to be given the time to participate in the planning workshops without being distracted by day-to-day activities. Good communication skills and a willingness to listen to others and participate respectfully in a team process are also important attributes for team members.

Beginning Scenario Planning

Once the question or focus of the scenario planning process has been determined and the team chosen, it is time to begin developing the scenarios. At a minimum, two meetings of the team should be scheduled: one to determine the driving forces for the scenarios and a second to review the story lines and develop strategies for the organization to use in addressing the identified issue. Depending on the time available, the group may want to hold two sessions on identifying factors that will have an impact on the future and additional meetings to determine possible strategies once the scenarios are developed.

At the first meeting, the planning team reviews the question and focus to be sure team members have a clear understanding of the issue to be addressed. Then the group identifies the key forces in the environment and trends that may have an impact on or influence the focal issue. The environmental analysis should identify social, technological, economic, environmental, and political trends and forces. Internally, the team should identify strengths, weaknesses, opportunities, and threats that will have an impact on the organization. Further, the group may want to look at forecasts about the future and consider which ones may be useful and which ones may limit the group's thinking. Local, city, state, and regional data sources can provide pertinent and valuable information for the group to consider.

Team members should exercise caution in using environmental scans from other organizations as the information may be dated or limited by the interests of the authors that produced them. Instead, team members can review the latest trend data provided by a variety of organizations in the library and information technology fields. Such organizations include, but are not limited to

- Gartner Inc., which conducts research on information technology and trends
- Ithaka S+R, which conducts research on the academic community and the transition to the digital environment
- NMC (New Media Consortium), which covers trends in education technology
- Educause, which looks at trends and developments in higher education technology
- Association of College and Research Libraries (ACRL), which can help identify trends having an impact on academic libraries
- International Federation of Library Associations and Institutions (IFLA), which represents the interests of library and information services and their users and tracks global trends in the information services field

The key element of this step, then, is for the group to think broadly about the environment and the future and not be limited by short-term forecasts.

Ranking the Forces and Choosing the Driving Forces

Now the team reviews the forces and trends and begins to categorize or rank the forces. Some forces, such as the aging of the Baby Boomer generation, will apply to all scenarios and thus will not help in the development of different scenarios or futures. Some forces will have high impact on the organization. These are the forces or trends that can fundamentally change the organization. Other forces will have a high degree of uncertainty relative to the key issue. These are the forces that make it difficult to predict the future. If team members agree on how a particular force will develop in the future, the force does not belong on the list of uncertainties.

From the list of most important forces and most uncertain forces, the team members choose the force or element in the environment that has the highest impact on the focal question and the force that is viewed as most uncertain. Each of these forces should be described on a continuum or on either/or axes to distinguish how they might impact the future. These two forces form the framework for developing four plausible scenarios.

Developing the Scenarios

The most important step in the scenario planning process is the choosing of the two axes that form the matrix for the scenarios (see figure 2.1). Each quadrant in the matrix becomes a scenario with a different view of how the future might develop. Team members use the trends and environmental factors identified in their meetings to outline how the future appears in each quadrant. Each story or scenario needs to be plausible. The scenarios should not be a best-case/worst-case dichotomy. Rather, the process should result in four unique versions of the future. It is helpful at this stage to outline the basic plot of each scenario and to assign a title to each scenario. Usually a few team members are given the task of developing the actual scenarios to bring back to the group for review. Chapter 4 provides more guidance on how to write the scenarios and develop plausible yet intriguing plot lines.

Determining the Implications of the Scenarios

Once the scenarios have been reviewed and the planning team agrees on how the four futures should be described, the team should look at the implications of each scenario for the organization and what strategies might be used by the organization as it prepares for an uncertain future. Remember that the scenarios are designed to help the organization make reasonable decisions in the face of uncertainty.

In developing strategies, questions for the team to consider are

- Are there themes that cross all four scenarios?
- Do the stories suggest particular issues that should be monitored?
- How will the organization need to change to be successful in any of these worlds?

A variety of strategies can emerge in the discussions of the scenarios. Some strategies will be applicable to all four scenarios. Some strategies may be most applicable to a few scenarios but neutral for others. Strategies may be helpful in one or two scenarios but more risky in the others. Some strategies may be ill-advised in all four scenarios. Identifying how the different strategies fit with the scenarios as well as with each other is an important part of the analysis process. The case study in chapter 9 provides an example of how to categorize strategies that the organization develops in the scenario planning process.

A Brief Example of Scenario Development

One example of how scenarios can be developed from a set of driving forces is found in the work of Tyler Walters. In "The Future of Knowledge Creation and Production in University Research Programs and Their Effect on University Libraries," Walters developed scenarios examining changes that could impact research programs at major universities.[13] He centered his work on the question "How will globalization and entrepreneurial approaches impact research program development in US universities over the next 15 years?" Based on his research and with input from university research offices, he identified major forces that impact research programs. These forces include

- increase in internationally based research funding
- changes in public funding for research and for research universities
- increased international competition
- entrepreneurial business model in place of research centers
- emphasis on public/private partnerships to carry out major research initiatives
- changes in public support for research universities
- increase in government regulations impacting research activities
- changes in regulations and laws covering intellectual property and copyright
- increases or decreases in international cooperation on "grand challenge" initiatives
- public and government demand that research data be available on the Web
- increases in multi-university-based research groups
- cyber infrastructure to support international cooperation and virtual environments

From these forces and after discussion with research offices, Walters chose two forces for the matrix. The most uncertain force was the culture of research institutions on a continuum from entrepreneurial research centers to more traditional academic departments. The most important force was the ability of US universities to remain competitive in the global environment on a continuum from *no longer competitive* to *remains competitive*. The matrix in figure 2.1 identifies the four plausible futures that can be identified from these driving forces.

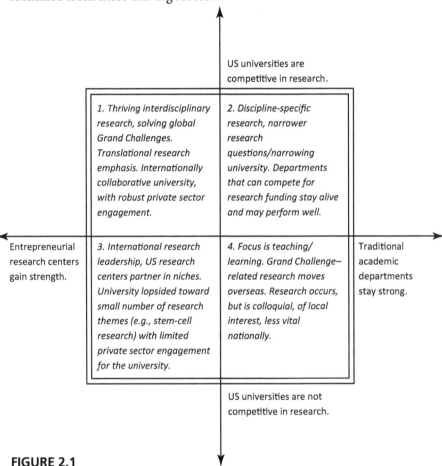

US universities are competitive in research.

1. *Thriving interdisciplinary research, solving global Grand Challenges. Translational research emphasis. Internationally collaborative university, with robust private sector engagement.*

2. *Discipline-specific research, narrower research questions/narrowing university. Departments that can compete for research funding stay alive and may perform well.*

Entrepreneurial research centers gain strength.

3. *International research leadership, US research centers partner in niches. University lopsided toward small number of research themes (e.g., stem-cell research) with limited private sector engagement for the university.*

4. *Focus is teaching/ learning. Grand Challenge– related research moves overseas. Research occurs, but is colloquial, of local interest, less vital nationally.*

Traditional academic departments stay strong.

US universities are not competitive in research.

FIGURE 2.1
Scenario axes. Source: Tyler Walters, "The Future of Knowledge Creation and Production in University Research Programs and Their Effect on University Libraries" (PhD diss., Simmons, 2013), 38–39.

Scenarios were written for each of the quadrants. The first scenario, "Thriving Interdisciplinary Research: Solving Global Grand Challenges," describes an environment where research centers dominate the research enterprise, academic departments play less of a role in research, and US universities remain competitive in the global research marketplace:

Scenario 1. Thriving Interdisciplinary Research: Solving Global Grand Challenges

GLOBAL CONTEXT

There are many robust research initiatives thriving on a global scale. They are aimed at solving many Grand Challenges* in research such as sustaining the environment (e.g., providing clean air and water), eradicating certain diseases, creating new biotechnologies, sustaining soils and agriculture, developing and sustaining renewable energy sources, and creating new information and communication technologies (ICTs) that rapidly evolve and reflect how individuals in a society work, entertain, and learn. A truly integrated global economy exists and demands some developments to improve societal conditions internationally as well as produce new goods and services that will serve as new economic engines. The global economy is healthy, yet is always looking for the next trend in goods, services, and technologies to sustain its growth. Governments, universities, private corporations, and private nonprofit research organizations have learned how to collaborate and fund research jointly to address the rising global challenges. They work together through national and international boards to determine the nature and priority of funded research agendas.

Many of the nations involved in the research initiatives have laws and regulations requiring that government-funded research is open globally after a one-year

---

*"Grand Challenges" (GCs) in research are defined by the National Science Foundation as being fundamental problems of science and engineering, with broad applications, whose solutions would be enabled by high-performance computing resources. It is also recognized that GCs also require extraordinary breakthroughs in computational models, algorithms, data and visualization technologies, software, and collaborative organizations uniting diverse disciplines (National Science Foundation Advisory Committee on Cyber infrastructure, Task Force on Grand Challenges, March 2011), p. xiv.[14]

period from the release of information and data. Governments recognize that global access is important; it may spur on innovation rapidly since many more researchers and private citizens will be able to work with the information. Corporations support the policy on open access to government-funded research since they have access to their competitors' research quickly and recognize that competitors may become collaborators in an upcoming research initiative.

US UNIVERSITY-BASED RESPONSE

Translational research is the focus, where findings diffuse from fundamental research to practical applications quickly. For many years, university-based research has remained too compartmentalized, based on academic domains. However, many universities and national governments in Europe, North America, Asia, India, the Middle East, South America, Australia, and New Zealand work together through interdisciplinary and transdisciplinary methods to optimize the diffusion. The world's leading research universities cultivate teams of researchers that contribute to these large-scale, internationally based research initiatives, many of which are funded for a decade. University administrators direct most internal resources and policy development toward fostering flexible and agile research organizations that gather the most renowned researchers from needed disciplines. These organizations work through an elaborate global network of researchers, constantly seeking new initiatives and associated funding. The university research groups collaborate internationally to respond to an agenda, apply for funding, conduct research, and spur the growth of the economies through private and public enterprises.

The universities, governments, corporations, and private nonprofit research organizations collaborate in developing and managing robust virtual community-based ICTs. They provide the cyber infrastructure required for the internationally connected university groups to collaborate, deliver research products, and work with private and public enterprises to translate findings into goods and services from which people, nations, and companies benefit. High-performance computing cycles are readily available and developed within international university- and government-based consortia. The research groups self-publish their research products (e.g., data, notes, commentaries, audiovisual media, reports, and publications) through their virtual research communities and other government-managed research repositories. They also use their universities' library-based publishing services to produce, disseminate, and manage their research products. The mix of corporate, government, and university researchers is changing constantly since the research funding goes to the best collection of researchers for a particular project.

This scenario describes an optimistic future where global cooperation and broad dissemination of research results dominate the research landscape. Universities using this scenario in planning might want to track how nations fund basic and applied research and how much emphasis is placed on transnational, interdisciplinary activities rather than on more narrowly focused national or institutional agendas.

Conclusion

Scenario planning provides decision makers with a structured approach for developing strategies to move the organization forward in uncertain times. The planning process, though, is flexible in that organizations can choose from a variety of models and steps to use in designing a system that will be effective for them. The process begins with the organization choosing a central point or decision to guide the discussions. Once the key focus area is determined, the decision makers explore the various forces that may be used to create a number of plausible futures. These futures or scenarios guide the development of strategies for the organization as it navigates through uncertainties and change. At times the discussions will be fuzzy and disorganized until a consensus is reached about the factors that are key to determining how the future might develop. The primary outcome of the process is a much broader understanding among decision makers of the issues that they will need to address if the organization is to be successful in coping with change. Scenario planning, then, helps organizations move from incremental change, which assumes the future will be the same as the present, to a more robust approach of addressing potential changes that could affect the success of the organization.

Notes

1. Peter Schwartz, *The Art of the Long View: Planning for the Future in an Uncertain World* (New York: Doubleday, 1991), 226–33.
2. Paul J. H. Schoemaker, "Scenario Planning: A Tool for Strategic Thinking," *MIT Sloan Management Review* 36, no. 2 (Winter 1995): 28–30.
3. Bill Ralston and Ian Wilson, *The Scenario Planning Handbook: A Practitioner's Guide to Developing and Using Scenarios to Direct Strategy in Today's Uncertain Times* (Mason, OH: Thomson Higher Education, 2006), 25.
4. Mats Lindgren and Hans Bandhold, *Scenario Planning: A Link between Future and Strategy* (London: Palgrave Macmillan, 2009), 39.
5. Ibid., 49.
6. Woody Wade, *Scenario Planning: A Field Guide to the Future* (Hoboken, NJ: John Wiley and Sons, 2012), 29.
7. David Mercer, "Simpler Scenarios," *Management Decision* 33, no. 4 (July 1995): 34, doi:10.1108/00251749510084662.
8. Thomas J. Chermack, *Scenario Planning in Organizations: How to Create, Use, and Assess Scenarios* (San Francisco: Berrett-Koehler, 2011), 68.
9. Shawn M. Keough and Kevin J. Shanahan, "Scenario Planning; Toward a More Complete Model for Practice," *Advances in Developing Human Resources* 10, no. 2 (May 2008): 168–69, doi:10.1177/1523422307313311.
10. Schwartz, *Art of the Long View*.
11. Ralston and Wilson, *Scenario Planning Handbook*.
12. Keough and Shanahan, "Scenario Planning," 169.

13. Tyler Walters, "The Future of Knowledge Creation and Production in University Research Programs and Their Effect on University Libraries," (PhD diss., Simmons, 2013).

14. Ibid., 44–46.

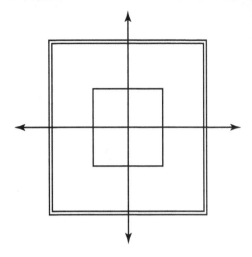

CHAPTER 3

WRITING SCENARIO PLOTS

Joan Giesecke and Deb Pearson

THE KEY INTEGRATIVE step in the scenario planning process is the creation of the stories or scenarios that incorporate the driving forces and factors in imaginative ways to describe different plausible futures. The stories are not simple extrapolations from the present based on known trends. Instead, the stories center on uncertainties to describe different ways that the future might evolve. The logic of the stories comes from the planning process. As noted in chapter 2, once the question or problem to be addressed in the planning process is defined, the planning group identifies the key driving forces, trends, and factors that can impact how an organization responds to the question at hand. From these driving forces, the group identifies the most uncertain forces and the most important forces to form a matrix to create four possible approaches to viewing the future. Each quadrant of the matrix becomes a scenario of a possible future.

To begin developing the scenarios, the group reviews the forces that are most relevant to a particular quadrant. The group also reviews the cause-and-effect trends that have an impact on the forces, hypothesizes possible events that might occur relevant to the scenario framework, and identifies possible conflicts that might occur. These elements become the foundation for the plot lines that are developed in each scenario. Next, the group should give each quadrant a brief, descriptive title that helps define the differences among the quadrants and therefore the differences among the scenarios. The titles should help readers quickly understand the essence of each scenario. The scenario writer then uses all this information to create the alternative stories of different futures that could develop.

Scenario Styles

Scenarios may be written in a number of styles. Some scenarios are character-based stories. Others are descriptions of events. All styles can be effective if the scenario captures the imaginations of decision makers and helps them see the future from a new perspective.

In *Fast Company*, Jamais Cascio described three styles of scenarios.[1] (Examples of each style are given in the sidebar.) In Scenario-as-History style, the tone of the scenario is not at all personal. Instead, it presents a dry account of the future. The writer can present the events that led up to the described future in more detail than is possible in the other two styles. This approach can be helpful as a way to explicitly connect the present to a possible future to help decision makers address events that may shape the future.

In a second style, Scenario-as-Story, the scenario is similar to a work of fiction with characters who operate in the described future. This scenario style has a number of advantages. The narrative form is familiar to readers and lets them quickly grasp the key elements of the plot. Readers should be able to relate to the characters and be comfortable with the action in the story.

The disadvantage of this style is that if the characters seem stereotyped or behave in extreme ways, readers may lose interest and dismiss the scenario as implausible.

Finally a third style is Scenario-as-Recollection. In this style, the writer describes the future with no pretense of a plot or story line. The scenario may be written in the first or the third person. It describes the thoughts of someone reflecting on the world of the scenario and how it differs from the past. The reader can understand the world described without having to believe in a set of characters.

No matter what style is chosen, every scenario should have certain characteristics:

- The goal of the narrative is to present ideas about a possible future that helps the reader examine events from a new viewpoint. It is not meant to actually predict the future.
- It is written in the present tense to make the possible future described seem more real and immediate.

- It describes a future that is plausible in relation to the issues and forces considered. It is not a veiled description of the present, a depiction of a preferred future, or a story too outlandish to be believed.

The group of scenarios centered on a particular issue should not describe a best-case/worst-case dichotomy. Rather, each scenario should present a different perspective on how the future might develop and what factors decision makers should monitor and address in their planning. Writers should avoid putting all the good news in one scenario and all the bad news in another; that approach will move planners to consider a preferred future instead of looking at a variety of plausible futures.[2]

EXAMPLES OF SCENARIO STYLES

In *Futures Thinking for Academic Librarians*, the authors provide twenty-six mini-scenarios of possible futures. It is possible to take any one of the scenarios and write it in each of the three styles. Using one scenario from that publication, "Everyone is a 'non-traditional' student," one can write three versions of the story.

Scenario-as-History

This is the style used in the publication Futures Thinking for Academic Librarians, *from which this text is taken.*[*]

Everyone is a "non-traditional" student. The interwoven nature of work/life/school is accepted in higher education as life spans increase and students are unable to fund tuition in one lump. Co-op education is widely embraced and faculty increasingly value students' life experiences. Knowing what the workforce wants, students are active in designing their own learning outcomes, and the personalized curriculum becomes the norm. Faculty evaluate students on demonstrations of learning—such as policy documents, marketing plans, or online tutorials—rather than old measures based on "seat time" and "credit hours."

---

*David J. Staley and Kara J. Malenfant, *Futures Thinking for Academic Librarians: Higher Education in 2025* (Chicago: American Library Association, Association of College & Research Libraries, June 2010), 12.

Scenario-as-Story

Sam has just transferred to State U to begin his junior year as a public administration major. He is excited and nervous to begin classes and to set up an internship as part of the co-op education program. He needs the work to help pay his tuition and the experience to prepare for full-time work when he graduates. He needs the work experience to help pay his tuition and to help him prepare for full-time work when he graduates. Sam meets with Jan, his advisor, who is also a librarian. Jan helps Sam find the courses he needs to tailor his program so he can find work in the public sector or at an NGO. Jan explains that his program will be a combination of online courses and face-to-face seminars. Jan also helps Sam review the co-op options that will be most helpful for his career. Sam tells Jan that he needs a program that leaves him time to be with his family. Jan assures Sam that finding a balance among work/life/school is one of the core values of State U. Jan also explains how the librarians can help him as he prepares projects and develops policy documents. Sam leaves the advising session reassured that he can make the transition to State U and fulfill his goals of a college degree that will get him a job and advance his career.

Scenario-as-Recollection

Jane, professor of public administration, looks out her office window at the quad at State U. How things have changed! No more are there groups of students relaxing on the lawn, meeting for coffee, or just hanging out. Instead, students coping with the challenge of paying for tuition and seeking a balance among school/life/work have little time for relaxing. Students are designing their own curricula to meet their career needs and are seeking highly competitive co-op positions to gain work experience and funding for school. Students are active participants in the planning process, are most likely to communicate with faculty and advisors electronically rather than face-to-face, and are personalizing the learning process to meet their own goals.

Major Plot Lines

Peter Schwartz, in *The Art of the Long View*, identified three main plot lines that can frame planning scenarios: winners and losers, challenge and response, and evolution.[3] These plots shape the actions of the characters or the organizations in the scenario stories. Which plot outline to choose will depend on the driving forces identified in the planning process and on the issue used to frame it.

Winners and Losers

In *winners and losers* plots, resources are perceived as scarce and conflict exists between characters or institutions. Writers of these plots will want to consider the role of power in the scenario and the potential development of alliances among the characters. Decision making in this plot approach can include political bargaining and compromise.

Challenge and Response

In *challenge and response* plots, the central characters or organizations face a challenge or test and respond to the events or forces. The responses can vary from optimistic approaches to more pragmatic or pessimistic approaches. Using a challenge and response approach can help decision makers move from a winner/loser view toward a problem-solving approach.

Evolution

In the *evolution* plot line, trends are believed to change slowly and incrementally. Decision makers have time to respond to changes and can design strategies to help the organization move slowly forward.

Other Plot Ideas

While the plot lines described above are the most common, according to Peter Schwartz, other plots may emerge in the scenario planning process. Some of the plots described below will fit well in an environment of rapid change and discontinuous trends.

Revolution

Plots that emphasize *revolution* examine times of radical change and the impact that change can have on the organization or characters in the scenario. The revolution must be plausible to be useful as a scenario plot. For example, natural disasters, political upheaval, or rapid technological change can frame a revolutionary plot line. While a plot centered on revolution can be frightening to decision makers, it can also help them think creatively about possible changes in their environment.

Cycles

As the name implies, *cycles* plots center on cyclical trends. Trends such as growth, development, and decline may be seen in scenarios focused on economic issues. The challenge for writers of these types of stories is to determine where in the cycle the organization is currently and what is the likely or plausible future cycle of activity.

Infinite Possibilities

Infinite possibilities is the most optimistic of the plot options. Here the organization anticipates continued growth and increased resources and prosperity. While this story line may be uplifting, writers need to be mindful that it still needs to be plausible to be helpful to decision makers. Assuming away all problems and then writing a story will not help decision makers develop reasonable strategies for the organization.

Lone Ranger

In the *Lone Ranger* plot, the individual is pitted against the system and strikes out on his or her own to address the focus issue. The individual may be either the hero or the villain in the story. Conflict between the individual and the organization becomes a key element in the plot. This type of plot line can help decision makers identify potential conflicts within the organization and possible negative reactions to proposed changes.

Writing the Story

The development of the scenario or the story includes both the planning group and a few individuals tasked with drafting the scenarios. The group reviews the driving forces identified in the scenario planning process and decides which factors should appear in any of the stories and which are uncertain and may vary between scenarios or stories. Analysis of the factors that have an impact on the planning question or topic helps the group determine the type of plot line that is likely to be used in each scenario. The group may also brainstorm possible events, time lines, or characters to be included in the scenario. These events, along with the approach or plot line, become the core of the story lines. Next, one or two individuals write the scenarios based on the results of the group planning processes.

One technique for writing scenarios is to begin with a one- or two-paragraph description of the future and then provide the two- or three-page story or narrative with details that relate to the description. Think of a scenario as a type of "Cliff Notes" or news story abstract with a commentary on events that shape the future. The plot should not be so elaborate that the focus on the key question is lost. The value of the scenario is in how well it helps decision makers develop strategies for coping with a changing environment, rather than in how entertaining or provocative it is.[4]

Good scenarios are usually no more than two or three pages, giving enough details for decision makers to be able to relate to the story but not including so many that they are distracted from the key points or view the stories as predictions of the future. The stories should be viewed as good fiction that helps people think creatively about the future. "The stories need to be familiar enough that readers can relate to the elements in the story but still suspend their current visions of the organization to see the future from a new viewpoint."[5] Scenarios should meet the three quality criteria noted by van der Merwe: quality scenarios are relevant, challenging, and plausible. They should address current concerns, be surprising enough to shift thinking, and be plausible in that they are "well-researched and provide detail and data to support the events in the story."[6]

Well-written stories have a number of characteristics. Each story should have a beginning, a middle, and an end that leads the reader to respond to a changed future. The story needs to be internally consistent so that the plot elements fall together into a coherent tale. There should be enough details for the reader to understand the forces that are in play in the scenario. The reader should be able to see how the forces and trends may interact. Some forces will be found in each of the scenarios developed as part of the planning process. Other forces will have an impact on only one or two of the plots. Each story should significantly stretch current perceptions, with at least one story including a major discontinuity to spark conversation about potential change.[7] Identifying the key differences among the stories is an important part of story writing so that readers can see how the described futures differ and react differently to each story. Although stories are describing a future state, they are written in the present tense as if the writer is in the future looking back and describing how that particular version of the future developed.

A variety of characters may be developed for the story and must relate to the key issue or question in the planning process. To create tension in the story and to move the plot along, protagonists and antagonists should be identified. Some of these characters will help in resolving issues, while others will be seen to block progress. Supporting characters help the main characters reach their goals. Together the characters bring emotions, and thoughts to the story and engage the reader in the narrative.

Once the initial drafts of the stories are completed, they should be circulated among the group members, who can suggest changes and improvements. Group members may identify errors in logic or implausible events or may find the scenarios not challenging enough. The group can use the quality assessment checklist developed by Thomas Chermack to evaluate the scenarios. Chermack identified the following characteristics of quality scenarios:

- Scenario titles are clever and easy to remember.
- Scenario stories are relevant, challenging, and plausible.
- Elements in the scenario are consistent and present integrated events.
- Managers can relate to the elements in the scenario.
- Scenarios encourage managers to experiment with different ideas.
- Scenarios include events that are meaningful.[8]

The scenario writers use the input from the group review to modify the stories and create scenarios that can be used in the planning process. Once the scenarios are written and reviewed, the planning process moves on to the creation of strategies and actions. These strategies and actions may apply to more than one scenario so that the organization can remain flexible and succeed in an uncertain environment and in times of change.

Conclusion

Storytelling is a powerful technique for organizations to use in planning in times of uncertainty and continuous change. Stories can capture the imagination of decision makers and help them see the world from a different perspective. Stories can be used to frame difficult conversations about change and to encourage looking beyond current trends and incremental change to addressing potential discontinuities in the future.

Well-written scenarios fulfill the purpose of encouraging flexibility in planning by providing a framework for the discussion of difficult issues and of possible rather than preferred futures. Successful scenarios are believable so that the reader is able to relate to the elements of the story. They can help advance the planning and reflection process. Poorly written stories that do not capture the imagination of the readers will leave the team with little to use in their planning process.[9]

Notes

1. Jamais Cascio, "Futures Thinking: Writing Scenarios," *Fast Company*, February 24, 2010, www.fastcompany.com/1560416/futures-thinking-writing-scenarios.
2. Louis van der Merwe, "Scenario-Based Strategy in Practice: A Framework," *Advances in Developing Human Resources* 10, no. 2 (May 2008): 234.
3. Peter Schwartz, *The Art of the Long View: Planning for the Future in an Uncertain World* (New York: Doubleday, 1991), 147–63.
4. Daniel G. Simpson, "Key Lessons for Adopting Scenario Planning in Diversified Company," *Planning Review* 20, no. 3 (May/June 1992): 16. doi:10.1108/eb054355.
5. Joan Giesecke, *Scenario Planning for Libraries* (Chicago: American Library Association, 1998), 32.
6. van der Merwe, "Scenario-Based Strategy in Practice," 232.
7. Simpson, "Key Lessons for Adopting Scenario Planning," 17.
8. Thomas J. Chermack, *Scenario Planning in Organizations: How to Create, Use, and Assess Scenarios* (San Francisco: Barrett-Koehler, 2011), 164.
9. Giesecke, *Scenario Planning for Libraries*, 33.

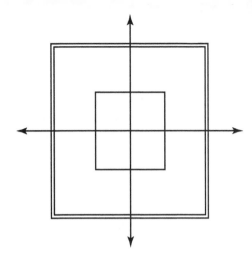

CHAPTER 4

DEVELOPING STRATEGIES FOR SCENARIOS

Joan Giesecke and Deb Pearson

THOUGHT-PROVOKING SCENARIOS ENCOURAGE decision makers to think more flexibly about the future. They are essentially a means to the end of letting decision makers think creatively about the organization. While the discussions of the stories or scenarios are valuable, the more lasting value of the process of scenario planning is the identification of both near- and long-term strategies for the organization. Scenarios help in the development of strategies for the organization in at least four ways.

First, scenarios help identify opportunities for the organization to consider new services or products. Second, scenarios may identify threats in the environment that can have an impact on the future of the organization and can help it make decisions about how to respond to those threats. Third, scenarios may suggest changes needed in the organization to respond to an uncertain future. And fourth, scenarios provide a way for an organization to test out ideas and to think about different strategies that may be useful as the future unfolds.[1]

Developing Strategies

Strategies are the means or plans that an organization uses to achieve a desired end. Strategies outline how resources will be allocated to achieve organizational goals and objectives. A good strategy includes the services or products to be delivered, the resources needed to accomplish the goal, the investment needed to achieve success, and an identification of key success factors. With these elements in place, an organization can implement a strategy to reach a desired end.

To begin the process of strategy development, the planning team should analyze the scenarios and identify success factors for each scenario. This analysis will show the common denominators of the scenarios and will also identify how the scenarios differ from each other. Planning team members can "rehearse" the scenarios by placing themselves each one, talking about the future depicted and what that future means to the organization. By exploring the stories in more depth, decision makers can identify the nuances that create the differences among the scenarios and explore how they, as decision makers, might act if the future develops as outlined in the scenarios.

From these discussions of the scenarios, there are a number of ways in which organizations can go about identifying possible strategies to use with the different scenarios or stories. One option is to conduct a group exercise using serious play. In serious play, members of the organization or planning team carry out a variety of creative tasks, from building models of the organization to analyzing museum artifacts, to inspire creativity. Using play can help decision makers identify politically sensitive issues, use metaphors and imagery to describe options, and move beyond thinking only in terms of facts and figures. In scenario planning, serious play can help decision makers think of new and bold ways to cope with uncertainty and uncomfortable futures.[2]

Another option is for decision makers to think in terms of robust and contingent strategies. Robust strategies are those strategies that can be used in any of the scenarios. These strategies tend to be short-term options to help the organization move forward. Contingent strategies are those strategies that fit under one or two scenarios but would be inadvisable under other scenarios. Contingent strategies may be good options to try as pilots or do as experiments with limited investment to test how well the strategy works as the future unfolds. Finally, decision makers can identify losing strategies. These are strategies that are ill-advised under any of the scenarios. These ideas present decision makers with plans to avoid and alert them to pitfalls that may derail the organization. In evaluating the various strategies, decision makers can ask if a strategy contributes to the desired direction of the organization, if it utilizes current strengths and assets, and if it matches the future environment. Strategies that meet all three criteria are most likely to succeed. An organization can then invest in robust strategies while experimenting with and allocating limited resources to contingent strategies that may work under some circumstances but could be disastrous in other futures. By identifying different types of strategies, the organization can move forward while evaluating changes in the future and hopefully decreasing the chances of missing opportunities that may develop over time.[3]

Decision makers can also use scenarios in evaluating current strategies to determine if the organization is poised to succeed in an uncertain future. Assessing current strategies gives decision makers an opportunity to reassess current planning to be sure that the organization is not completely committed to a set of strategies that is built on the idea that the future will be similar to the present with minimal change and minimal uncertainty. They can identify potential threats that may not have been considered when strategies were first proposed as well as position the organization to exploit potential opportunities that may have been missed in more traditional planning processes. Decision makers may find that current organizational strategies become losing strategies if there is any uncertainty in the future or if the organization faces unanticipated changes. Scenario planning discussions then provide decision makers with an opportunity to think about uncertainties in the future as well as assess current plans to be sure that the organization is poised to move forward no matter how the future develops.

Displaying Strategies

There are a number of ways organizations can list out potential strategies for evaluation by the planning team. One process is to create a table with the strategies listed in the first column and the four scenarios forming the headings of the next four columns. Then team members can identify which strategies fit with each of the scenarios as shown in table 4.1.

In the book *Shaping the Future: Advancing the Understanding of Leadership*, four students in the Simmons managerial leadership doctoral program presented a set of scenarios analyzing possible futures for children's programming in public libraries.[4] The four scenarios are set in a medium-sized suburb of Chicago in a public library system with three branches and a central library in the downtown area. The town is facing an economic downturn, and the public library is concerned about ongoing support. In reviewing the issues, the most important force was determined to be the motivation of the staff and the most uncertain force was the level of community support. From these two forces, four scenarios were developed to explore possible changes that might occur in the children's program in five years.

The complete scenarios are reported in the book *Shaping the Future.*[5] Each scenario includes possible strategies that the public library might employ if the future begins to develop as outlined in the scenario. While listing strategies at the end of each scenario is one way to provide decision makers with options, a more effective way to present strategies to decision makers is to provide a comparative table that helps decision makers evaluate the strategies in relation to the various scenario options.

With the scenarios on children's programming, one possible comparative analysis of the individual strategies is presented in table 4.1.

Using this visual display, decision makers can engage in discussions of the various strategies and how these options might fit with current strategic plans for the organization. In those discussions, they may revise the table, deciding that strategies developed during the scenario planning process might not be appropriate given the environment or that strategies may be effective in more or fewer scenarios. The discussion of options can help decision makers ensure that they are thinking about uncertainties that might impact the organization.

Conclusion

As described in chapters 1 and 2 of this volume, scenario planning processes help decision makers look creatively at the future and allow them to assess possible strategies for advancing the organization in times of uncertainty. Scenario planning processes also help decision makers avoid some of the pitfalls in decision making that can have an impact on organizations. According to Thomas Chermack, scenario planning has the potential to address a number of core causes for decision failure, including

- bounded rationality, or the inability of decision makers to consider all feasible alternatives
- failure to consider external and internal variables
- mental models that limit how decision makers view their organization[6]

Table 4.1
Comparison of possible strategies in response to four scenarios on the future of a library system's programming for children.

Strategies	Scenarios			
	1. Dirty Dozen Low Staff Motivation Low Community Support	**2. Beauty and the Beast** Low Staff Motivation High Community Support	**3. Pollyanna and Her Friends** High Staff Motivation High Community Support	**4. The Little Engine That Could** High Staff Motivation Low Community Support
Develop a new strategic plan.	X			X
Develop a new vision statement.	X			X
Use Appreciative Inquiry to obtain staff input on strengths and weaknesses.	X			X
Schedule children's programming during adult programs such as resume-writing workshops.	X			
Partner with schools and day care centers to provide children's programming.	X	X	X	X
Reinvigorate Friends Group to raise funds.	X	X	X	X
Use volunteers to provide children's programming.		X	X	

Table 4.1

Comparison of possible strategies in response to four scenarios on the future of a library system's programming for children.

Strategies	Scenarios			
	1. Dirty Dozen Low Staff Motivation Low Community Support	**2. Beauty and the Beast** Low Staff Motivation High Community Support	**3. Pollyanna and Her Friends** High Staff Motivation High Community Support	**4. The Little Engine That Could** High Staff Motivation Low Community Support
Rotate children's librarians from main library to branches.	X	X		
Partner with local college for students to do children's programming.	X	X		
Apply for grants for children's programming.	X	X	X	X
Work with other city departments to share resources.			X	
Conduct public relations campaign to engage community.	X			X
Provide diversity training to staff.			X	
Expand technology to support online homework options.			X	
Survey community to identify needed library services.	X			X

Scenarios help decision makers overcome these barriers in a number of ways. Scenarios help minimize bounded rationality by encouraging more creative approaches to looking at alternatives or strategies to help the organization. The stories of plausible futures provide different contexts for the organization to consider in assessing strategies and making decisions about future plans. The scenario planning process brings both external and internal variables into the discussion of the future by looking at the forces that are having or may have an impact on the organization. Assessing the impact of these forces and determining the most uncertain and the most important trends and forces for the organization will expand how decision makers assess their options. Finally, creation and discussion of various plausible futures and the scenarios or stories that describe those futures help create new mental models or alter current mental models so that decision makers become more flexible in looking at the future.

The scenario planning process brings systems thinking into the decision making process. Systems thinking is the process of seeing interrelationships and patterns of change. In systems thinking, individuals shift from seeing parts of the organization to seeing the whole organization, from being helpless reactors to active participants in shaping reality, and from reacting to the present to creating the future.[7] In scenario planning, systems thinking begins with defining the question to be addressed, moves to assessing the forces having an impact on the organization, continues with the creation of scenarios, and finally brings decision makers together for the development of strategies for the organization to use in organizational planning. The process provides organizations with options for planning and developing strategies to improve the chances of success in times of change and uncertainty.

Notes

1. Bill Ralston and Ian Wilson, *The Scenario Planning Handbook: A Practitioner's Guide to Developing and Using Scenarios to Direct Strategy in Today's Uncertain Times* (Mason, OH: Thompson Higher Education, 2006), 139–40.
2. Loizos Heracleous and Claus D. Jacobs, "Developing Strategy: The Serious Business of Play," in *Business Leadership: A Jossey-Bass Reader*, 2nd ed., ed. Joan Gallos, (San Francisco: Jossey-Bass, 2008), 330–32.
3. Joan Giesecke, *Scenario Planning for Libraries* (Chicago: American Library Association, 1998), 22.

4. Peter Hernon, *Shaping the Future: Advancing the Understanding of Leadership* (Santa Barbara, CA: Libraries Unlimited, 2010), 187–98.
5. Ibid.
6. Thomas J. Chermack, "Improving Decision-Making with Scenario Planning," *Futures* 36, no. 3 (April 2004): 306–7. doi:10.1016/S0016-3287(03)00156-3.
7. Peter Senge, *The Fifth Discipline: The Art and Practice of the Learning Organization* (New York: Doubleday, 1990), 69.

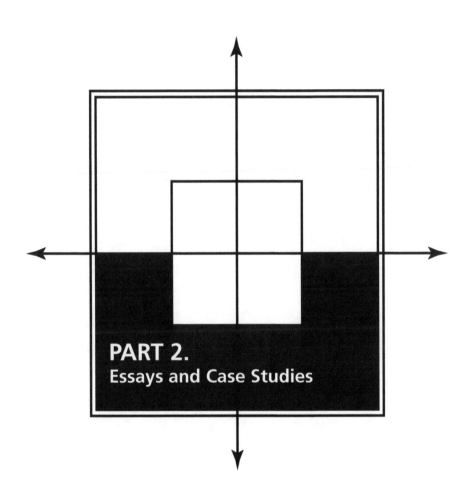

PART 2.
Essays and Case Studies

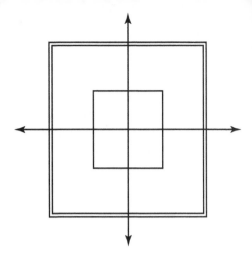

CHAPTER 5

USING COMPLEMENTARY RESEARCH METHODS TO ENHANCE SCENARIO PLANNING

Tyler Walters

Introduction

ORGANIZATIONS USING SCENARIOS in their strategic planning can at times find it difficult to tailor them to their own situation, thus making the scenarios less meaningful to their own specific contexts. Reading and discussing scenarios and how one's organization may respond to a scenario can be a useful component of any strategic planning initiative. However, using additional research techniques can help to expand and deepen an organization's understanding of its strategic directions. This essay provides guidance on how planners and planning teams can use a variety of techniques to enhance the planning process.

As discussed in part I of this book, scenarios are stories about possible future environments in which organizations will operate and how they will adapt to achieve their missions. Scenarios offer plausible stories representing the consequences of external forces, usually economic, technological, political, and cultural. Institutions and organizations can use these stories for strategic planning. However, strategic planning that uses scenarios coupled with additional research techniques can aid in making the scenarios more rigorous as well as yielding more understanding from them. This chapter examines three such techniques: the *Delphi method, semi-structured interviews,* and *case studies.* The Delphi method can be used in interviewing experts to elicit relevant information as scenarios are built. Semi-structured interviews are appropriate for gathering information from stakeholders to help shape scenarios. Semi-structured interview methods help planners design questions of significance in research and allow an interviewer to alter the order and nature of the questions based on the interviewee's responses. The case study method can be used after the scenarios are drafted. Planners interview stakeholders about the scenarios and create case studies based on their feedback. Examination of the case studies can help focus plans for an organization's response to the scenarios. This chapter also delves into the differences between the use of scenarios in planning and the scenario planning process and discusses how additional research techniques can enhance planning by providing planning teams and decision makers with additional data to consider in evaluating future strategies.

In part I of this guidebook, the authors offer a framework for developing scenarios for libraries. Using this framework reveals key forces driving a selected phenomenon and identifies the most uncertain factors shaping those forces over the next fifteen years. This approach creates descriptions of possible futures to which libraries can respond through strategic planning. Scenario development is commonly based on a matrix derived from the identified key forces and most uncertain elements (see chapter 2). Detailed descriptions of each scenario, or stories, are written to illuminate and illustrate the traits found in each quadrant of the matrix. Mietzner and Reger offered additional criteria for good scenarios:

- *Plausibility:* Each scenario is likely to happen.
- *Differentiation:* The scenarios differ from one another, and, as a group, they postulate several futures.
- *Decision-making utility:* Each scenario provides insight that assists future planning.
- *Challenge:* Each scenario challenges traditional perceptions of the future.[1]

According to Martino, accurate and successful planning with scenarios has a limited time frame.[2] His research has shown that fifteen years represents the limit of predictability and that the accuracy of predictions declines beyond this period. Martino was an early proponent of using the

Delphi method, explaining that it is a structured group communication approach used to gather feedback from individuals, who usually are separated geographically. The method involves designing questions to elicit responses from experts who help the planner to refine understanding of a certain phenomenon or to refine written scenarios. The question and feedback process is anonymous and places the planner in control of the flow of information.

The approach described in part I, in conjunction with Mietzner and Reger's scenario criteria and Martino's approach to applying the Delphi method, ensures the development of meaningful scenarios that are useful for planning purposes.

Scenario Planning versus Using Scenarios

There is a difference between using scenarios in planning and conducting scenario planning. However, this author has seen much confusion between the two in the field where real organizations plan. Many organizations use scenarios in strategic planning but do not create their own scenarios. Instead, they use scenarios written for other purposes or have scenarios developed for them by an external source. Most scenario-related activities described in reports and literature are of this type. In using scenarios, libraries generally focus on interpreting and applying existing scenarios. They may also solicit feedback from experts and stakeholders on externally written scenarios and adapt one or more of them.

Scenario planning, on the other hand, focuses on creating sound and reliable scenarios. The validity and usefulness of the scenarios developed in any organizational planning initiative are determined by the research methods used to gather the data that informs the scenario writing process. Scenario planning and using scenarios developed by others are two sides of the same coin, if you will; in both cases, the rigor of the process must be given careful consideration if strategic planning based on scenarios is to have a positive effect on an organization's development.

Research Methods

This section looks at how to use the Delphi method, the semi-structured interview method, and the case study method effectively in creating and evaluating scenarios. It also discusses the use of stratified and purposive sampling methods to choose the participants from whom feedback will be sought.

Delphi Method

The RAND Corporation created the Delphi method beginning in the 1950s, when it used the method to aggregate a wide range of opinions about future environments and circumstances to tailor a response. The goal of this method is to remove independent, subjective information or opinion and find objective trends and commonalities. In particular, planners employ the Delphi method where data and information do not yet exist or are extremely difficult or expensive to obtain.[3]

The Delphi method is a "method for structuring a group communication process so that the process is effective in allowing a group of individuals, as a whole, to deal with a complex problem."[4] It collects the opinions of individual experts for the purposes of setting a framework for future organizational decisions and direction. The experts may be separated geographically; they also remain anonymous to each other throughout the process.

The Delphi method uses questions designed to capture quantifiable answers. A panel of experts receives the questions in successive rounds, usually a minimum of two. The process described here has three rounds:

- The planning team drafts scenarios and then creates questions about the draft scenarios, asking for quantifiable answers. The questions are distributed to a panel of experts.
- The experts individually review the questions and the draft scenarios and return their feedback.
- The planning team summarizes the answers, updates the draft scenarios based on the feedback, and adds other information it considers relevant. It then distributes the material to the experts for a second round.
- The experts update or add to their answers to the original questions and provide feedback on the efficacy of the revised scenarios.
- The planning team uses the feedback to further refine the draft scenarios and sends them to the experts for a third round of review.
- The experts provide their final feedback on the scenarios.
- The planning team creates the final draft of the scenarios.

In addition, although consensus is not a requirement of the Delphi method, the planning team looks for any points of consensus in the interviewees' responses and takes particular note of those points in revising the scenarios.

In every round of the process, the planning team asks the questions of each expert individually so that the opinion of other experts and persuasive interaction between them are not factors to consider when analyzing the answers. The techniques deployed in the Delphi method have been found effective and generally accurate.[5] In fact, the Delphi method can be up to 95 percent reliable for future forecasting.[6]

Semi-structured Interview Method

The semi-structured interview method is helpful in gathering insights from a library's decision makers and other stakeholders in response to draft scenarios. As explained by Beck and Manuel, the semi-structured interview method is one in which the planner designs the questions to probe the interviewees' lifeworlds—the sum total of their physical environment and everyday experiences. Planners "must allow their respondents to express themselves fully in order to study those worlds."[7] Planners can then use the insights gained in this process to help shape the scenarios.

Wildemuth also put forth guidelines on semi-structured interviews.[8] The interviews are conducted one-on-one between the planner and the interviewee. The method starts with a fixed list of questions to be asked in a particular order, as do structured interviews; however, it allows for variations in the questioning process in the midst of the interview. Wildemuth states, "Semi structured interviews give the interviewer considerable freedom to adjust the questions as the interview goes on and to probe far beyond a particular respondent's answers to the predetermined questions."[9] For instance, an interviewer, anticipating the possibility of the interviewee's wanting to expand on a given answer, may follow up a response with a question different from the next one on the list. The semi-structured interview method gives the interviewer the ability to probe the interviewee's perspective and follow particular points as they arise during the interview, which allows the interviewer to collect a more in-depth set of narrative data.

In preparation for a semi-structured interview, the planning team should send the draft scenario and questions to the interviewee in advance so that the live interview will elicit the best, most thought-out answers. The team may also want to encourage interviewees to share the draft scenario and interview questions with their direct reports to gather feedback. Thus, responses given in the interview will include the views of the interviewee and other stakeholders in that library department. During the interview, the interviewer may want to take notes and record the conversation, so interviewees should be asked to consent to recording and note taking in advance. After the interviews are completed and before the interview information is used to draft or revise scenarios, the planner should listen to the recorded interviews and compare them to the notes. In addition, the planner should ask each interviewee to review the interview notes to ensure that they accurately reflect that person's ideas. By having two interactions with each interviewee, having the interviewees gather responses from their associates, and consulting both notes and interview recordings while drafting or revising the scenarios, the planner develops a methodological triangulation to corroborate the research findings.[10]

The semi-structured interview process can also be applied to drafting and revising case studies and plans in response to scenarios.

Case Study Method

Deriving case studies from scenarios can augment the scenario story and help a library in tailoring its response. A case study analyzes "an organization, individual, or event and the external and internal forces acting upon it."[11] That analysis is descriptive and sometimes attempts to explain the set of circumstances having an impact on the organization, individual, or event. Yin provided an excellent case study development process that can be used with scenarios.[12] In fact, by using multiple case studies—one per scenario—libraries can examine how to design and implement their services in response to the scenarios. By further analyzing the case studies, libraries can identify the similarities and differences in the interviewees' responses, analyze the scenario forces and their impacts on the libraries in their institutional settings, and determine how specific conditions provoke a library's response. A cross-analysis of the set of case studies can also yield a more in-depth description of the issues faced and more unique insights than the examination of any single case study. Case study research allows the planning team, and subsequently the case study readers, to understand organizational environments, contexts, and drivers and how they affect the organization, as well as the individuals working within the organization, through a comprehensive narrative description and examination.[13]

Semi-structured Interview Method in Case Study Construction

Planning teams should consider which research methods they will use to gather feedback from stakeholders about the scenarios that is appropriate and germane to building in-depth, specific case studies from the scenarios. Using the semi-structured interview method, a planner can collect interviewees' responses to structured questions and then analyze them and incorporate them into two rounds of questions and revised versions of the case studies. The interviewees review and comment on the case studies during these two rounds. The first-round responses focus on reviewing the scenarios' key force and the main element of uncertainty. After the first round of responses, the interviewees each review the first complete draft of the case study and provide feedback on its accuracy and appropriateness. The planner then incorporates their feedback into a second draft of each case study. The interviewees are given an opportunity to review the second draft and provide feedback. The planner then incorporates this second round of feedback into the final version of each case study. This process is much the same as the semi-structured interview process used to create scenarios described earlier, just applied to constructing case studies.

A modified approach to developing case studies from scenarios is to have interviewees read only one of the scenarios, the one most favored by the people interviewed for their construction. This approach allows planners to explore the most likely scenario in depth, resulting in more complete findings directly applicable to current and emerging organizational settings. The scenario interviewees can also assist the planning team in identifying the less likely and less desirable scenarios. As a result, libraries may be able to spend less time and energy planning for them. Having case study interviewees focus on and respond to only the most favored scenario helps the planning team to concentrate its research and consider the most likely organizational directions, strategies, and outcomes.

Planning teams may also want to compare the case studies stemming from a particular scenario with different interviewees, who can help the team identify general similarities and differences between the cases related to the main areas being considered, such as services, infrastructure, or human and financial resources. Examining differing approaches among the cases may also help planners better understand the particular strategic directions being adopted by an organization. Moreover, such comparisons can also illuminate the issues being faced by the organization and the trends developing as the organization grows and evolves as described in the scenario.

Using the case study method in developing scenarios helps planners understand how institutions like universities, colleges, and academic libraries will respond to the scenarios. The semi-structured interview process can elicit questions, comments, and perspectives about scenarios that were not considered during their initial development. These new perspectives can be incorporated into a case study, further illuminating how study participants interpret the scenarios as their implications are considered. Hence, scenario-based case study development extends the usefulness of scenarios, creating a view of how single institutions can develop strategies to succeed in various future environments and providing *real-world* feedback about the likelihood of the scenarios themselves.

Stratified and Purposive Sampling

Before using any of the research methods described above, the planning team has to determine which institutions and persons will be invited to participate. Stratified sampling is one approach that works well in selecting interviewees for both scenario and case study construction. Stratified sampling is the "grouping of the units composing a population into homogeneous groups (or strata) before sampling."[14] Such a method improves the representativeness of the study sample. The planners can stratify either organizations or individuals into these homogeneous divisions prior to choosing which to invite to participate in the research and conducting the interviews.

Purposive sampling can also be applied to determine organizations and individuals that are prime representatives to participate in a given research project. The planner selects individuals or organizations she or he considers most appropriate for the study, relying "on the expert judgment of the person selecting the sample."[15]

In some cases, stratified and purposive sampling can work together. For instance, once the stratified categories are set up and potential participants identified, purposive sampling may be used to select which possible interviewees will be asked to participate. In addition, a planner can consult others who have knowledge of the research topic and of the potential interviewees and their organizations to help determine the final participants.

Both the stratified and purposive sampling techniques can strengthen case studies and a library's response to them.

Conclusion

The strength of using scenarios in planning lies in the capacity of scenarios to incorporate well-grounded and verifiable outside forces into a story through which a library can begin to plan and respond to these external factors. The amount of scientific and methodological rigor used in developing scenarios will have a direct impact on their quality and accuracy, and hence on the quality and accuracy of the library's response to the scenarios. Utilizing other research methodologies, such as the case study method, can facilitate and structure an organization's planning and preparation for a given scenario and add more rigor and consistency to the process. In addition, semi-structured interviews and specific sampling techniques also introduce more consistency and rigor into the research and planning process. Moreover, these additional research methods add value to the overall practice of using scenarios in planning, rendering it a more credible and reliable strategic planning scheme.

Notes

1. Dana Mietzner and Guido Reger, "Advantages and Disadvantages of Scenario Approaches for Strategic Foresight," *International Journal of Technology Intelligence and Planning* 1, no. 2 (2005): 233.
2. Joseph P. Martino, "The Precision of Delphi Estimates," *Technological Forecasting* 1, no. 3 (March 1970): 293–99, doi:10.1016/0099-3964(70)90030-X.
3. Jon Landeta, "Current Validity of the Delphi Method in Social Sciences," *Technological Forecasting and Social Change* 73, no. 5 (June 2006): 467–482, doi:10.1016/j.techfore.2005.09.002.
4. Harold Linstone and Murray Turoff, *The Delphi Method: Techniques and Applications* (Reading, PA: Addison-Wesley, 1975), 3.
5. Gene Rowe, George Wright, and Andy McColl, "Judgment Change during Delphi-like Procedures: The Role of Majority Influence, Expertise, and Confidence," *Technological Forecasting and Social Change* 72, no. 4 (May 2005): 377–99, doi:10.1016/j.techfore.2004.03.004.
6. Frederick J. Parente, Janet K. Anderson, Patrick Myers, and Thomas O'Brien, "An Examination of Factors Contributing to Delphi Accuracy," *Journal of Forecasting* 3, no. 2 (April/June 1984): 173–82, doi:10.1002/for.3980030205.

7. Susan Beck and Kate Manuel, *Practical Research Methods for Librarians and Information Professionals* (New York: Neal-Schuman, 2008), 70.

8. Barbara Wildemuth, *Applications of Social Research Methods to Questions in Information and Library Science* (Westport, CT: Libraries Unlimited, 2009).

9. Ibid., 233.

10. Robert K. Yin, *Case Study Research: Design and Methods* (Los Angeles: Sage, 2014).

11. US General Accounting Office, *Case Study Evaluations* (Washington, DC: General Accounting Office, 1990).

12. Yin, *Case Study Research.*

13. US General Accounting Office, *Case Study Evaluations.*

14. Earl R. Babbie, *The Practice of Social Research,* 13th ed. (Belmont, CA: Wadsworth Cengage Learning, 2012), 212.

15. Ibid., 190–91.

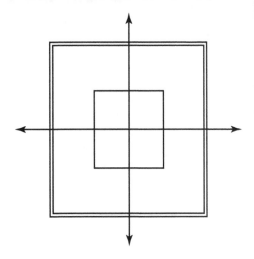

CHAPTER 6

SCENARIOS ON HIGHER EDUCATION

Tyler Walters

SCENARIOS HELP DECISION makers consider contradictions and uncertainties in planning for the future. Further, scenarios help them challenge conventional wisdom by exploring plausible, yet different, possible futures. Royal Dutch Shell Corporation, which, as discussed in chapter 1, began using scenarios in the 1970s, is one of the largest corporations that continues to develop and use scenarios to explore changes in technology, the environment, population, and energy. The corporation shares its scenarios via its website, and they are used by government agencies and industry experts in determining strategic options for future development.[1] These scenarios can be particularly helpful to academic libraries as they consider the changes that will have an impact on higher education. Libraries can also turn to a variety of scenarios that have been developed specifically for higher education, and for academic libraries in particular, to enhance their strategic planning efforts by expanding the traditional environmental scanning process to include the examination of possible futures.

International Higher Education Scenarios and Research Programs

A variety of agencies on the international level have developed scenarios about higher education to explore possible futures in times of change. Scenario-developing studies in Scotland and England are prominent examples.[2] A few notable examples from the continent of Europe and from other areas of the world exist as well. Significant European examples have been produced by the European Commission and by researchers from the University of Twente Center for Higher Education Policy Studies in the Netherlands.[3] The Organisation for Economic Co-operation and Development, with member countries around the globe, has produced research with an international focus.[4] Universities in other countries that have western-style economies and a large population of English speakers, such as South Africa and Malaysia, have undertaken in-depth scenario development exercises as well. Thirteen South African universities participated in the scenario-creation efforts of SARUA (Southern African Regional Universities Association), published in 2012, and the Universiti Sains Malaysia (University of Science, Malaysia) compiled a 2007 report that included five scenarios about the future of higher education in Malaysia.[5]

Although they look at higher education, most of these efforts do not directly address the questions of most concern to academic libraries. They generally do not investigate how universities will organize research programs or how the identified drivers will shape the universities for the long term. They make only cursory remarks about how research will be organized and conducted in the future, noting action steps such as participating in grid-based research or joining the Internet2 Consortium. Nevertheless, these international studies provide insights into how other countries plan to develop their higher education infrastructure. General recommendations related to research reflect national aspirations: for example, predicting that Malaysian universities will become regional R&D hubs or that universities in southern Africa will "contribute to socio-economic innovation and development."[6] However, these studies do not explain why becoming a regional leader in research is desired, let alone describe how research will be conducted, organized, and funded at the university, national, or regional level.

Most international higher education scenario planning focuses on identifying and describing the drivers to upcoming higher education development. The shared key interest in these scenario efforts is in furthering the education of the national or regional populations to sustain and drive their economies. In fact, the chief concern is economic development, not academic research program development. The national- and regional-level planning initiatives thus focus on trends in areas such as information and communications technology and public policy as they relate to the national economy.[7] Internationalization is also a major theme because the planners desire to understand its impact on national and regional economies and, in turn, on higher education and the need for a skilled workforce.[8] One study highlighted "human capacity" as a main driver—that is, having enough skilled people to develop the higher educational system and maintain the national economy.[9] The purpose of many of these studies has been to relate higher education to economic transition and sustainability. For US and Canadian libraries, these insights may help them anticipate changes in the global information environment where issues of sustainability and economic data are addressed.

International Scenario Drivers

The international scenario planning efforts commonly identify several driving forces and elements. The identified higher education drivers tend to be those that have significant impact on the economies of the countries and regions.

The theme of *international integration* in higher education appears in the "global university" scenario, where universities openly cooperate and collaborate across national borders and have well-defined linkages for technology transfer between universities and industry.[10] Other scenarios describe the "open university," where internationalization of education occurs between universities and rarely involves corporate interests.[11] Research is described in global university scenarios, albeit briefly, but only because organizational leaders were attempting to put together the best researchers to address an identified research challenge and provide solutions.[12]

Technology is also a widely used axis in scenario planning for higher education. Study authors regularly want to forecast how widely available and how highly developed information technology will be.[13] There is an attempt to rationalize higher education investments and expenditures on technology as a way to maximize the impacts of teaching, learning, and research. Current studies have focused on how to achieve this within the European Union or in southern Africa.

Privatization of higher education as well as *public-private partnerships* in the public university setting are common drivers. Some scenario authors have gone as far as developing scenarios for "Higher Education, Inc.," the "corporate university," and the "differentiated university landscape," announcing that the for-profit higher educational institution is a fixture in the upcoming higher education landscape.[14] Other studies have developed a three-tiered approach to higher educational institutions: (*a*) a small cadre of research-intensive universities, (*b*) many "grand universities" that conduct both research and teaching and learning, and (*c*) the private, for-profit university that meets the needs of the national population to acquire knowledge and skills.[15] These studies acknowledge a growing role for private, for-profit higher educational organizations as well as the internationalization of higher education in general through more coordination, especially in the European Union. The bifurcation of higher educational systems is a commonly expressed outcome because of the identified drivers. Future scenarios divide universities into research-intensive versus teaching-and-learning-intensive institutions.[16] When university research is described in such a scenario, it is typically divided, with government funding basic research, and private, for-profit corporations funding applied research.[17] However, scenario authors tend to focus on the system level and do not detail future changes at the level of a single institution. They also focus on the university's teaching and learning role and rarely address changes to research programs within the universities.

Other predominant scenarios appearing in several planning reports are in complete contrast to the open and global university scenarios. These scenarios describe universities that *meet local community educational needs and remain state-run*.[18] Still others describe scholar-led universities that *essentially remain the same* as they have in past decades and centuries, where the university serves learning for learning's sake. There is accountability to funding agencies; however, the university is autonomous and sustained.[19] In the European Commission report, Haegeman describes a most desirable scenario of a *"knowledge triangle"* in which universities, governments, and private entities come together and work in harmonious coordination to further knowledge acquisition and discovery across the EU nations.[20] Other scenarios offered include the "à la carte university," which is student-led and *market-driven*, meeting the educational needs of students anytime, anywhere. In a related scenario called the "invisible university," universities are market- and technology-driven. They follow a highly decentralized organizational model, much like the community-driven, open-source software model, and they serve students' educational needs as determined in the open marketplace.[21]

North American Scenario Studies of Higher Education

Only one North American scenario study of higher education exists as of 2014, conducted by the ten-campus University of California system.[22] One other example is from the University of Arizona and its brief scenario planning documents.[23] Neither of the scenario-related efforts in these two states addressed research, nor did either provide the axis-based key driving forces and uncertain elements from which the scenarios were derived. The University of California report provided a system-wide vision and strategies to guide the university system toward 2025.[24] It looked at the state's changing demographics, its economics, the poor condition of its K–12 educational system, the undergraduate and graduate educational needs of its people, the research needs of California, the state's place in a global society, and the continued growing financial challenges facing higher education and California in general. The UC study serves much the same purposes as its foreign counterparts, that is, to identify a vision and strategies to develop a robust economy and an educated workforce.

The four scenarios put forth by the UC study are these:

1. *Beyond the Tipping Point:* Financial support for UC comes too late, and academic programs degrade precipitously.

2. *Virtuous Circle:* California's economy roars back, with renewed public investment in UC, which will be in a position to make economic improvements by increasing the educated populace and making new scientific discoveries in its research related to common world problems.

3. *UC Polytechnic:* The state provides more money for its K–12 schools, which then better prepare high school graduates for college in California.

4. *Complementary Campuses:* State funding continues to decline, but UC is able to grow its teaching and learning and research programs by adopting strategies similar to those of other university systems across the globe: the UC campuses specialize, creating unique centers of excellence in research, yet all strive for excellence in undergraduate education. This approach is complementary, not overlapping or duplicating research efforts.[25]

The University of California chose scenario four to use in creating strategies for the system. The main strategies in the fourth scenario are to create unique centers of excellence and to coordinate and collaborate internationally. Perhaps the leading example of this strategy is the California Institutes for Science and Innovation, described as an "unprecedented three-way partnership between the state, California industry, and the University of California."[26] The Institutes also work directly on research initiatives with several universities in China, and the authors pointed out that the relationship between California and China is economically significant and culturally and historically salient. This research arrangement is reminiscent of the European Commission's "knowledge triangle" scenario.[27]

The University of Arizona's documents referring to the use of scenarios and scenario planning provided even fewer details regarding its research program and did not mention the library. The most recent described two polarized scenarios: "Celebrating Tradition" and "Organizational Metamorphosis."[28] The report stated that the first scenario is "one of maintaining traditional values and approaches while doing what is necessary to survive the present; the future is assumed to be a series of relatively consistent incremental changes and a continuation of the current vision." The second scenario acknowledged that "the world has changed and the university needs to make major changes in both the short term (driven by financial constraints) and the long term (guided by strategic choices)."[29] The Arizona documents focused mostly on the state-level political landscape and positioning the University of Arizona well within it. They did not address transitions in research program development or any internationalizing components.

International Scenario Studies of University Research Trends

Two of the international scenario studies delved into the future characteristics of university research programs and internationalization and thus may be of particular interest to academic libraries. The University of Twente study, led by Enders and his colleagues, provided some commentary on organizing research activity in each of three scenarios.[30] The study focused on Europe and acknowledged a global context, noting that academic research and development can and may be transferred to other regions, such as Asia, Latin America, or South Africa. None of the authors commented on US or Canadian research universities or the role of university libraries; however, chapter 5, describing a scenario set in 2020 called "Octavia, the

Spider-Web City," did discuss organizing research initiatives in cross-institutional teams with diverse funding sources:

> Most [research universities] have organised their research in inter-faculty and inter-university units that are comprised of flexible and semi-permanent teams in self-organised centres with control over, and responsibility for, costs and revenues. Face-to-face contact with partners interested in knowledge transfer forms the basis for cooperation with business and increasingly with other organizations and interest groups. Strategic alliances, the in-sourcing of private R&D, and mixed university-company campuses are organisational responses to the new mix of funding opportunities, changing university research missions and novel research technologies. Academics themselves are the major players and drivers of these developments towards a greater overlap between the realms of academia and the commercial world.[31]

And chapter 6, a description of the 2020 scenario "Vitis Vinifera, the City of Traders and Micro Climates," stated:

> "Big science" is increasingly undertaken by cross-national tailor-made consortia that draw on top university based researchers and their counterparts from the public and private sectors. Despite a number of expensive ERC programmes to encourage European research networks, the self-perception and scientific practice of Europe's leading centres continues to be unashamedly international. Exclusive European networks are seldom those at the cutting edge.[32]

These two scenarios illustrate ways to organize research programs differently and explain how internationalization in particular can drive their transformation.

The report from the Organisation for Economic Co-operation and Development (OECD) also included scenarios on research directions with an international perspective.[33] Chapter 5, by Stéphan Vincent-Lancrin, which was based on an examination of research program development in member countries from the 1980s to the 2000s, offered four axis-based scenarios: (*a*) open collaboration, (*b*) national interest promotion, (*c*) international research marketplace, and (*d*) new public management.[34] The chapter discussed the occurrence of a "massification of academic research," meaning that the amount of academic research conducted was up massively over the twenty-year period addressed by the study.[35] Vincent-Lancrin also indicated that there was a 52 percent increase in research articles in the sciences and social sciences from 1988 to 2005 among OECD member nations (the data include the United States and Canada).[36] In addition, from 1981 to 1999, the OECD countries experienced a 127 percent growth in the number of university researchers.[37] Given that Vincent-Lancrin conducted the research across all of OECD's thirty member nations in Europe, Asia, Oceania, and North and South America, the trend of increased research production, scholarly articles, and personnel indicates a growing internationalization in research activity.

Vincent-Lancrin's chapter also discussed several other characteristics of academic research organizational transition. Traditionally, research universities have been known for producing basic research. However, Vincent-Lancrin's research indicated that nonacademic sectors such as government agencies, nongovernmental organizations (NGOs), and private corporations also perform basic research.[38] Thus, research universities are asking if basic research, as opposed to applied and industry-based research, is where they want to focus their resources. Vincent-Lancrin also posited a scenario for OECD countries called the "new public management." In this scenario, there is less public university funding, and sources of private funding are growing rapidly; however, through government regulation, these private resources are monitored closely and are expected to serve societal needs to produce highly educated and skilled national populations and research results of high societal value.[39] The described scenario is reminiscent of the current environment at public research universities in the United States and Canada. Vincent-Lancrin claimed that heightened governmental regulation is a new driver for higher education and research development and offered another new, major driver: technology in the form of "new computing and networking opportunities."[40] Moreover, the chapter asserted that research trends will support open, international collaboration and an international research marketplace where funds for research are sought, national interests within certain research sectors are promoted, and there is a new "social contract" between public and private interests to fund and regulate research activity.[41]

The scenarios and related information in the University of Twente report and in Vincent-Lancrin's chapter in the OECD report set the context and suggest likely drivers for librarians to consider as they contemplate using scenarios in planning.[42]

University Library–Related Scenario Studies

Since approximately 2009, many library-related scenario development and planning studies have been conducted. Librarians and researchers have undertaken scenario development to examine future roles for the Federal Depository Library Program (FDLP) in university research libraries and in public libraries.[43] Other studies have looked at future roles for digital libraries, academic health science libraries, and scholarly communication.[44] Still others have examined the future of the book and of publishing services in university libraries.[45] There has even been a scenario study looking at the future of higher education and academic libraries' roles within it.[46] This last study, conducted for the Association of College and Research Libraries (ACRL), presented twenty-six possible scenarios for academic libraries in the year 2025. The authors stated, "The scenarios represent themes relating to academic culture, demographics, distance education, funding, globalization, infrastructure/facilities, libraries, political climate, publishing industry, societal values, students/learning, and technology."[47] The ACRL study did not address the theme of research specifically, but it referenced the future of the research process and stated that libraries must adapt: "Libraries will need to reconsider what their relevance is in the research process. We need to start considering what our 'deeper meaning' is to researchers to ensure that we fit into this new model. I feel strongly that we will have a role; it will look different from our role now, and we need to be careful not to cling to past practice for nostalgic reasons."[48] While this quote highlights the changing environment—the transforming academic research process and libraries' role within it—the study itself did not offer specific scenarios, strategies, or roles for libraries to consider while planning.

Two scenario-based planning initiatives within academic library communities attempted to focus on future research directions, translating them into paths of development for library services. Both were meant to serve as guiding documents for libraries engaging in strategic, long-range planning, but one was not based on rigorous scenario development research.

The first, based in the United Kingdom, is known as the Libraries of the Future project (LotF). It was sponsored by the British Library, the Joint Information Systems Committee (JISC), Research Libraries UK, the Research Information Network, and the Society for College, National, and University Libraries. The project's report focused on how different types of higher education institutions interact (research-intensive, teaching-and-learning-focused, and private, for-profit) and how they interact with government, private corporations, and regional economic groups and industries.[49]

The scenarios describe the future legal, technological, economic, and governmental environments in which research takes place in the United Kingdom as well as how librarians and library services may evolve to support future research projects. The LotF project's scenarios focus on the national (UK) level and more on whether higher education institutions will be private institutions operating in the marketplace or state-controlled entities with a mission dedicated to the common good. The report also focuses on whether institutions of higher education will be relatively open, available to a broad section of the population for learning purposes, or closed and rather elitist, carefully guarding their educational offerings and research products that they see as unique, having financial value, and thus protected as intellectual property.

The Association of Research Libraries (ARL) developed scenarios relating to academic research during 2009–2010.[50] The ARL and a group of its member library directors designed the scenarios and an associated toolkit for use by member libraries in their strategic planning as they transition in response to certain driving forces affecting university research (i.e., social, technological, economic, and political/regulatory environments). The scenarios focus on whether the research enterprise is aggregated (controlled by disciplines, countries, or institutions) or diffused (left up to individuals and loosely coupled organizations of a virtual or location-based

nature) and whether individual researchers are constrained or uncon-
strained by resources, technologies, policies, and their own creativity. The
scenario overviews describe the larger milieu in which researchers perform research, followed by fictional stories casting an individual researcher
in each scenario. *The ARL 2030 Scenarios* is useful because the scenarios
take a global view of where research may be growing and shrinking nationally and regionally. They also capture the perspectives of library directors
on research program development because library directors served as the
study population in ARL's scenario development work. The scenarios comment substantively on the nature and sources of research funding and tend
to focus on the experience of the individual researcher in the larger scenario environment. However, they do not look at how the institutional setting
of the research university itself may change because of the scenarios and
how, within the university, transitions in research program development
and organization might occur.

A number of ARL libraries have used *The ARL 2030 Scenarios* in their
organizational planning processes. As reported in ARL's *Research Library
Issues*, using scenarios developed outside the organization can prove to
be challenging.[51] Because the scenarios did not address the role of the research library within each scenario environment, participants in planning
processes struggled to relate the *2030* scenarios to local conditions. The
libraries found that the staff did a good job of looking for early indicators
for each of the scenarios. However, they were less successful in identifying
strategies that would work across all four scenarios. The libraries reported
that the scenarios generated lively discussions and helped staff think more
creatively about possible roles for their libraries in a changing research environment.

Tips for Using Higher Education Scenarios

Higher education and research library scenarios can help generate discussions among library staff about the changes and uncertainties they are likely
to face in the future as they design services to support the research mission
of their institutions. To facilitate the discussion and help staff understand
how scenarios developed outside of their environment, discussion leaders
can create a set of questions to help guide the discussion. Questions about
early indicators that might signal that a particular scenario could happen
can help staff relate to the stories. Facilitators may also want to review the

case studies and questions posed in Woody Wade's book *Scenario Planning: A Field Guide to the Future.*[52] This book provides a variety of questions and approaches that can be used with scenarios to challenge staff to think beyond incremental changes and consider discontinuities and uncertainty in the development of strategic initiatives as part of the planning process.

Notes

1. For information on Royal Dutch Shell scenarios, see www.shell.com/global/future-energy/scenarios.html.
2. Ahmed Abd El Ghaffar, Katrin Alberding, Vasily Nicholsky, and Anaken Lai, *Scenario Thinking: Vision 2020* (St. Andrews, UK: St. Andrews University Press, 2005); Jeroen Huisman, Harry de Boer, and Paulo Charles Pimental Botas, "The Future of English Higher Education: The Changing Landscape" (unpublished manuscript) www.utwente.nl/mb/cheps/publications/Publications%202011/LFHE%20Changing%20landscape%20paper%20final%20edit%20JH.pdf.
3. Karel Haegeman, *The Future State of Higher Education in Europe: Mini-scenarios for 2025* (Seville, Spain: European Commission, January 25, 2011), www.edu2025.ro/UserFiles/File/IPTS.pdf; Jürgen Enders, Jon File, Jeroen Huisman, and Don Westerheijden, eds., *The European Higher Education and Research Landscape 2020: Scenarios and Strategic Debates* (Enschede, The Netherlands: University of Twente, Center for Higher Education Policy Studies, 2005), www.utwente.nl/bms/cheps/publications/Publications%202005/Enders05european.pdf.
4. Organisation for Economic Co-operation and Development, "Six Scenarios for Universities" (discussion paper, OECD/CERI Experts Meeting on "University Futures and New Technologies," Washington, DC, January 12, 2005), excerpted from Stéphan Vincent-Lancrin, "Building Futures Scenarios for Universities and Higher Education: An International Approach," *Policy Futures in Education* 2, no. 2 (2004): 245–62, www.oecd.org/edu/skills-beyond-school/36758932.pdf; Organisation for Economic Co-operation and Development, "Four Future Scenarios for Higher Education" (paper, OECD/France International Conference, Higher Education to 2030, Paris, France, December 8–9, 2008), www.oecd.org/education/skills-beyond-school/42241931.pdf; Organisation for Economic Co-operation and Development, *Higher Education to 2030, Volume 2: Globalisation* (Paris: OECD Publishing, 2009), www.mfdps.si/Files//Knjiznica/higher%20educational%202030%20OECD.pdf.

5. Southern African Regional Universities Association, *Building Higher Education Scenarios 2025: A Strategic Agenda for Development in SADC*, SARUA Leadership Dialogue Series, vol. 3, no. 2 (Johannesburg, South Africa: SARUA, 2012), www.sarua.org/files/publications/SARUA%20leadership%20Dialogue%20Series/Leadership%20Dialogue%20Series%20Vol%203%20No%202.pdf; Universiti Sains Malaysia, comp., *Constructing Future Higher Education Scenarios: Insights from Universiti Sains Malaysia* (Pulau Pinang: Universiti Sains Malaysia, 2007), http://globalhighered.files.wordpress.com/2010/08/con_future.pdf.

6. Universiti Sains Malaysia, *Constructing Future Higher Education Scenarios*; Southern African Regional Universities Association, *Building Higher Education Scenarios*, 37.

7. Abd El Ghaffar et al., *Scenario Thinking*.

8. Ibid.

9. Southern African Regional Universities Association, *Building Higher Education Scenarios*, 37.

10. Haegeman, *Future State of Higher Education in Europe*, 12–14.

11. Ibid., 15–17.

12. Ibid.

13. Abd El Ghaffer et al., *Scenario Thinking*.

14. Organisation for Economic Co-operation and Development, "Four Future Scenarios"; Haegeman, *Future State of Higher Education in Europe*; Universiti Sains Malaysia, *Constructing Future Higher Education Scenarios*.

15. Huisman, de Boer, and Botas, "Future of English Higher Education."

16. Ibid.

17. Organisation for Economic Co-operation and Development, *Higher Education to 2030*.

18. Ibid.; Universiti Sains Malaysia, *Constructing Future Higher Education Scenarios*.

19. Universiti Sains Malaysia, *Constructing Future Higher Education Scenarios*.

20. Haegeman, *Future State of Higher Education in Europe*.

21. Universiti Sains Malaysia, *Constructing Future Higher Education Scenarios*.

22. University of California, *UC 2025: The Power and Promise of Ten* (Sacramento: University of California, 2006), www.universityofcalifornia.edu/future/lrgt1106.pdf (page now discontinued).

23. Roger Caldwell, "Two Scenarios for the University of Arizona in 2025," University of Arizona, January 28, 2009, http://cals.arizona.edu/dean/planning/rlc-ua-scenarios-jan09.pdf.

24. University of California, *UC 2025*.

25. Ibid., 19–20.

26. Ibid., 33.
27. Haegeman, *Future State of Higher Education in Europe.*
28. Caldwell, "Two Scenarios for the University of Arizona."
29. Ibid, 2–3.
30. Enders et al., *European Higher Education and Research Landscape.*
31. Jürgen Enders, Frans Kaiser, Henno Theisens, and Hans Vossensteyn, "Octavia, the Spider-Web City," in Enders et al., *European Higher Education and Research Landscape,* 82–83.
32. Jon File, Eric Beerkens, Liudvika Leišytė, and Carlo Salerno, "Vitis Vinifera, the City of Traders and Micro-Climates," in Enders et al., *European Higher Education and Research Landscape,* 92–93.
33. Organisation for Economic Co-operation and Development, *Higher Education to 2030.*
34. Stéphan Vincent-Lancrin, "What Is Changing in Academic Research? Trends and Prospects," in Organisation for Economic Co-operation and Development, *Higher Education to 2030,* 173–78.
35. Ibid., 147.
36. Ibid.
37. Ibid.
38. Ibid., 151.
39. Ibid., 153–57.
40. Ibid., 147.
41. Ibid., 164.
42. Enders et al., "Octavia, the Spider Web City"; File et al., "Vitis Vinifera, the City of Traders and Micro-Climates"; Vincent-Lancrin, "What Is Changing in Academic Research?"
43. Peter Hernon and Laura Saunders, "The Federal Depository Library Program in 2023: One Perspective on the Transition to the Future," *College and Research Libraries* 70, no. 4 (2009): 351–70; Cynthia Chadwick, Renee DiPilato, Monique le Conge, Rachel Rubin, and Gary Shaffer, "The Future of the FDLP in Public Libraries," *Public Libraries* 51, no. 4 (July/August 2012): 40–47.
44. S. N. Vignesh, "The Future Scenario of Digital Library Era," *SRELS Journal of Information Management* 46, no. 1 (March 2009): 25–28; Logan Ludwig, Joan Giesecke, and Linda Walton, "Scenario Planning: A Tool for Academic Health Sciences Libraries," *Health Information and Libraries Journal* 27, no. 1 (March 2010): 28–36; Marie Carpenter, Jolie Graybill, Jerome Offord Jr., and Mary Piorun, "Envisioning the Library's Role in Scholarly Communication in the Year 2025," *portal: Libraries and the Academy* 11, no. 2 (April 2011): 659–81, doi:10.1353/pla.2011.0014.

45. David J. Staley, *Futures Thinking for Academic Librarians: Scenarios for the Future of the Book* (Chicago: Association of College and Research Libraries, May 2012); Tyler Walters, "The Future Role of Publishing Services in University Libraries," *portal: Libraries and the Academy* 12, no. 4 (October 2012): 425–54, doi:10.1353/pla.2012.0041.

46. David J. Staley and Kara J. Malenfant, *Futures Thinking for Academic Librarians: Higher Education in 2025* (Chicago: Association of College and Research Libraries, June 2010).

47. Ibid., 3.

48. Ibid., 10.

49. Geoff Curtis, Claire Davies, Max Hammond, Rob Hawtin, Gill Ringland, and Chris Yapp, *Academic Libraries of the Future: Scenarios beyond 2020* (Academic Libraries of the Future Project, 2011), http://www.foresightfordevelopment.org/sobipro/download-file/46-79/54

50. Association of Research Libraries and Stratus, Inc., *The ARL 2030 Scenarios: A User's Guide for Research Libraries* (Washington, DC: Association of Research Libraries, October 2010).

51. Ludwig, Deborah and Jennifer Church-Duran, "Scenario Planning: Developing a Strategic Agenda for Organizational Alignment," *Research Library Issues*, no. 278 (March 2012): 8, http://publications.arl.org/rli278.

52. Woody Wade, *Scenario Planning: A Field Guide to the Future* (Hoboken, NJ: John Wiley and Sons, 2012).

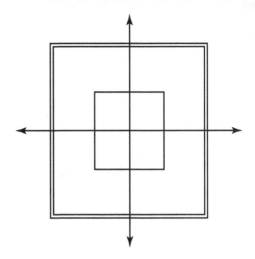

CHAPTER 7

HOW SCENARIOS HELP ORGANIZATIONAL LEADERS THINK CREATIVELY ABOUT CHANGE

Jon Cawthorne

UNIVERSITY RESEARCH LIBRARIES will continue to face institutional, technological, and societal changes for the foreseeable future. As a result, library leaders must think realistically about how to move strategically toward a desired future, one where all resources are used effectively and the university library can demonstrate its value to the twenty-first-century academic institution. Scenarios can be an important planning tool for leaders to use in times of uncertainty and change. Scenarios help leaders and organizations to consider increasing uncertainty, expand current thinking, and improve long-term decision making The scenario planning process described in this book is designed to avoid the influence of current organizational cultures and structures, legacy research library collections, and ingrained services. Scenarios thus help libraries to rethink their services, thereby moving beyond the image of the traditional research library.

Developing a vision is the first step for the library leader to take in moving the current organization toward a successful future. In times of societal, cultural, economic, and technological changes, library directors are challenged to articulate a well-thought-out strategic vision that considers increasing levels of uncertainty and clarifies plausible future directions for the university research library. Next, leaders need to assess the current organizational culture to identify barriers to achieving the strategic vision. Finally, leaders choose strategic scenarios for the planning process. The scenarios need to relate to the strategic vision, address issues of culture, and introduce new ideas about possible directions for the organization.[1]

Staley and Malenfant suggest that to help librarians and other staff relate to the strategic scenarios and the library director's vision and be willing to accept needed changes, leaders can ask the following questions:

- "If this scenario were to exist today, would we be able to leverage it to our advantage?"
- Are the "resources, staffing, organizational processes, and strategies" available "to take advantage of this scenario?"
- "If this scenario were to exist today, in what ways are we currently vulnerable to the change it represents?"
- "To what degree" do the strategies in the scenario and the underlying values of the organization leave our library leaders unprepared or "unable to respond effectively to the conditions this scenario represents"?
- If all the necessary staffing and resources were available, "what could we do to leverage this scenario to our advantage"?
- "What would need to happen—internally and in the external environment—for this vision to become a reality?"[2]

All these questions are critical when library directors think about incorporating scenarios into current or future planning efforts. They also suggest changes that may be needed in the current organization.

For example, the second question above begins to ask what "resources, staffing, [and] organizational processes" are in place today to prepare for future scenarios. The last question introduces the need to assess the internal organizational culture as well as external factors.

Defining Culture and Development of Groups

Research is beginning to show that organizational culture is less a permanent, manifested phenomenon and more a manipulated asset.[3] Academic library leaders can use scenarios to expand their views of the organizational culture; the fundamental perceptions, beliefs, and patterns of behavior and norms; and the in which librarians and other staff make sense of their environments.[4] Thus the way library directors use scenarios can contribute to new organizational culture norms and beliefs. In turn, these new norms and beliefs can foster new thinking and approaches to change in the research library. Identifying the right changes to organizational structures and culture moves the library closer to the strategic scenarios. Yet before well-intentioned change initiatives begin, library directors must understand the culture that governs collective group action. Developing this ability to be aware of unseen forces at work in the organization requires library directors to understand how their vision resonates with library culture or cultures and how groups develop over time.

Edgar Schein, one of the first researchers to define and write extensively on organizational culture, stated

> The bottom line for leaders is that if they do not become conscious of the cultures in which they are embedded, those cultures will manage them. [Therefore], cultural understanding is desirable for all of us, but it is essential to leaders if they are to lead.[5]

He defined culture as

> A pattern of shared basic assumptions learned by a group as it solves its problems of external adaptation and internal integration that works well enough to be considered valid and therefore may be taught to new members as the correct way to perceive and think and feel in relation to those problems.[6]

The explanation of shared basic assumptions and modifying work to externally adapt and internally integrate fits the research library culture. As directors and others in the university research library confront the challenges of positioning the library, it becomes important to adapt externally to the environment and to integrate new thinking and possibilities that might run counter to existing perceptions. And, as Schein's definition suggests, once the culture is established, new people who come into the organization are taught how to think and feel about problems facing the organization.

In a slightly different approach, Alvesson and Sveningsson referenced seven characteristics that describe culture as the elements that stand behind and guide the behavior of individuals and groups in organizations. They described these characteristics as follows:

- Culture is holistic and refers to phenomena that cannot be reduced to single individuals; culture involves a larger group of individuals.
- Culture is historically related; it is an emergent phenomenon and is conveyed through traditions and customs.
- Culture is inert and difficult to change; people tend to hold on to their ideas, values and traditions.
- Culture is a socially constructed phenomenon; culture is a human product and is shared by people belonging to various groups. Different groups create different cultures, so it is not human nature that dictates culture.
- Culture is soft, vague and difficult to catch; it is genuinely qualitative and does not lend itself to easy measurement and classification.
- Terms such as "myth," "ritual," "symbols," and similar anthropological terms are commonly used to characterize culture.
- Culture most commonly refers to ways of thinking, values and ideas of things rather than the concrete, objective and more visible part of an organization.[7]

As a socially constructed phenomenon, culture involves ways of thinking and the unspoken values that govern how people in the organization interact with one another. These "myths," "rituals," and "symbols" show that a culture is (*a*) a learned entity, (*b*) a belief system, (*c*) a strategy, and (*d*) a perspective reflecting mental programming.[8] Understanding the idea that culture can be viewed as a strategy is a key for library directors in understanding deeper aspects of groups. For Schein, this belief system evolves as the group evolves. Groups evolve from forming the group, to building the group identity, to working effectively as a group, to reaching a new level of maturity as a group. Through these stages, the group changes from depending on the leader for decisions, to accepting group members and promoting harmony, to learning to work effectively together, to focusing on preserving the group and its culture.[9]

These four stages, Schein believes, are the raw material around which a group organizes itself to accomplish its task and create a viable, comfortable organization. Every group must solve the problems of member identity, common goals, and mechanisms of influence, and the leader must understand the transition between stages of group development from *dependence* to *maturity* (e.g., from "The leader knows what we should do" to "We know who we are, what we want, how to get it. We have been successful, so we must be right."). The process of changing a culture takes years, and, despite long-held assumptions that organizational cultures do not change easily, Fortado and Fadil showed that leaders can have influence on it.[10]

Leadership for Change

Cameron believes that changing organizational culture is difficult, and research shows that culture is still largely unrecognized.[11] Further, commonly shared interpretations, values, and patterns are difficult to modify once they are set. While it is difficult to change an organization's culture, according to Cameron, there are seven steps that organizations can take to begin the change process. (Note the usefulness of scenarios in the third step.)

1. *Clarifying meaning:* "The first step is to clarify what it means and what it does not mean for the organization's culture to change. Moving toward one particular type of culture does not mean that other culture types should be abandoned or ignored."[12] Clarifying meaning also requires understanding the subcultures on the campus and in the library. For instance, as library directors learn the campus culture, they also have to recognize staff subcultures.

2. *Identifying stories:* "Since organizational culture is best communicated through stories, a second step is to identify one or two positive incidents or events that illustrate the key values that will characterize the organization's future culture."[13]

3. *Determining strategic initiatives:* Scenarios can be particularly useful during this step. Because scenarios are designed to take into account uncertain elements in the environment—possibly more than the organization did in previous strategic planning—using them can help the organization develop more effective, future-oriented strategic initiatives.

4. *Identifying small wins.* "The rule of thumb regarding small wins is to find something easy to change, change it, and publicize it. Then, find a second thing easy to change, change it, and publicize it. Small successes create momentum in the desired direction, inhibit resistance—since seldom do people resist small, incremental changes—and create a bandwagon effect so that additional supporters get on board."[14]

5. *Crafting metrics, measures, and milestones.* "Change requires the identification of indicators of success in culture change as well as interim progress indicators. A data gathering system needs to be designed as does a time frame for evaluating the results."[15]

6. *Handling communication and symbols.* "Explaining why the culture change is necessary and beneficial is probably the most vital step in generating commitment."[16] When, where, and how to communicate the ideas for new work as described in the strategic scenarios are critical decisions that the library director makes in the culture change process.

7. *Developing leadership:* "All organizational change requires leadership, champions, and owners. Culture change does not occur randomly or inadvertently in organizations, and it requires leaders who are consciously and consistently directing the process."[17]

As the next decades bring ongoing change to institutions, the university research library will need leaders who can articulate a vision and take actions that begin to change organizational cultures. By doing so, leaders encourage flexibility in staff and develop processes to identify new skill sets for staff if their organizations are to succeed.[18]

Conclusion

University research libraries make a substantial investment in human resources. Scenarios offer a way to challenge the assumptions, beliefs, and ways of seeing in the organizational culture. Every culture requires leaders to have a vision. However, for long-term sustainable progress toward the vision, the library director must also have a greater understanding of the organizational culture within which decisions are made. As a result of the continuing trend of increasingly limited resources and greater accountability at institutions, more library directors will need to become leaders who strategically realign staff and create conditions that generate innovation in library services.[19] Scenarios are an invaluable tool for such leadership efforts.

Notes

1. Jon Edward Cawthorne, "Viewing the Future of University Research Libraries through the Perspectives of Scenarios" (PhD diss., Simmons, 2013).
2. David J. Staley and Kara J. Malenfant, *Futures Thinking for Academic Librarians: Higher Education in 2025* (Chicago: Association of College and Research Libraries, June 2010), 21–22.
3. Bruce Fortado and Paul Fadil, "The Four Faces of Organizational Culture," *Competitiveness Review* 22, no. 4 (2012): 283–98.
4. Carol Shepston and Lyn Curries, "Transforming the Academic Library: Creating an Organizational Culture That Fosters Staff Success," *Journal of Academic Librarianship* 34, no. 4 (July 2008): 358–68.
5. Edgar Schein, *Organizational Culture and Leadership*, 3rd ed. (San Francisco: Jossey-Bass, 2004), 14.
6. Ibid., 17
7. Mats Alvesson and Stegan Sveningsson, *Changing Organizational Culture: Cultural Change Work in Progress* (New York: Routledge, 2008), 36.
8. Shili Sun, "Organizational Culture and Its Themes," *International Journal of Business and Management* 3, no. 12 (2008): 137–41.
9. Schein, *Organizational Culture and Leadership*, Page 70
10. Fortado and Fadil, "The Four Faces of Organizational Culture."
11. Kim Cameron, "A Process for Changing Organizational Culture," in *Handbook of Organizational Development,* ed. Thomas G. Cummings (Thousand Oaks, CA: Sage, 2008), 429–45.
12. Ibid., Page 437
13. Ibid., 438
14. Cameron, "A Process for Changing Organizational Culture," 9. Page 439.
15. Ibid.

16. Ibid.

17. Ibid., Page 440

18. David W. Lewis, "A Strategy for Academic Libraries in the First Quarter of the 21st Century," *College and Research Libraries* 68, no. 5 (September 2007): 430.

19. Michael A. Crumpton, "Strategic Positioning for Staff Realignment," *Bottom Line* 25, no. 4 (2012): 143–48; Ronald C. Jantz, "A Framework for Studying Organizational Innovation in Research Libraries," *College and Research Libraries* 73, no. 6 (November 2012): 525–41, doi:10.5860/crl-302.

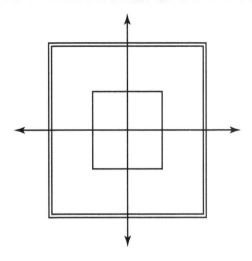

CHAPTER 8

SCENARIOS FOR PLANNING WITH HUMAN RESOURCE DIRECTORS

Jon Cawthorne

THE PACE OF technological change in and around the university research library is steadily increasing. As library directors consider their institutional environments and align their visions with established organizational cultures, missions, and available resources, planning becomes increasingly important. In the planning process, it is critical to use tools that broaden, develop, or refine a vision. As library directors find the balance between identifying the right roles for the library and new skills needed in the future university research library, they require new planning tools that help them develop a vision and articulate different futures to provosts, presidents, and other library colleagues. More and more, the implementation of this vision needs to factor in the significant personnel resources in the library. Scenarios offer just such a planning tool and allow directors a chance to articulate a strategic vision, rethink their organizational structures, and develop a plan specific to their institution's environment, mission, and direction.

As directors think about the future, they should focus on more than operational needs. Changing the current university research library requires identifying future directions amid uncertainties. Ideally, directors will use tools that integrate future thinking and encourage strategic decision making into the day-to-day planning of their organizations.[1] With academic, institutional, and political environments changing, academic library directors must develop, communicate, and rely on a strategic vision to secure funding, support a changing academy, and rally or motivate others to achieve the desired change. Scenarios help them understand and clarify driving forces that become key factors in developing a leadership vision.

This chapter reports on four case studies that looked at how library human resource directors differed in their analysis of a set of scenarios on the future of academic libraries. While previous studies of the use of scenarios in academic libraries and institutions have included the perspective of the library director, no studies have examined the role of the human resource director in addressing uncertainty and change in the libraries.

The full research study included the development of four scenarios that were refined by library directors from members of the Association of Research Libraries.[2] The author used a combination of interviews and Delphi techniques (see chapter 5) to gather input and refine the scenarios. The final scenarios are presented in this chapter. The author then did in-depth interviews at four research libraries to compare the viewpoints of provosts, library directors, and human resource directors. The results of the case studies presented below concentrate on the viewpoints of the human resource directors and highlight the impact that the different perspectives of the interviewees could have on the libraries as the libraries implement changes in staffing to meet the needs of an uncertain future.

The Importance of Human Resource Directors

In all libraries, personnel costs comprise a major share of budgets. The costs represent a significant investment in hiring, training, and developing personnel to provide library services. More importantly, as the next decade brings new changes to institutions, the university research library will need both flexibility from its staff and a process to identify new skill sets needed to succeed.[3] In his article on staffing, James Neal recognized the need for academic library directors to become more sensitive to the diverse backgrounds, interests, and aspirations of new professionals. Directors then balance the aspirations of new professionals with the staffing needs of the organization. With or without the ability to hire new staff, library directors must lead transformative change and avoid the incremental staffing decisions that address only specific, temporary needs in units or departments. The future success of academic libraries depends on the director's ability to encourage librarians and other staff to navigate the ambiguous definitions of what it means to be an academic librarian. With a large number of librarians expected to retire in the next decade, this is an opportune time to reshape the library staff in dramatic fashion.[4]

The transformation of academic libraries requires developing anew the human resource structures within the university research library.[5] As Stephens and Russell explained,

> Every person working in a library has a unique contribution to make toward the success of the organization, provided that person is committed to the mission of the library and his/her values are consistent with organizational values. Many of the skills employees bring to the job are never utilized. More and more employees today (but not all) seek to be fully engaged in the organization and its mission and to use their skills and knowledge in the workplace. At the same time, organizations are beginning to recognize the tremendous untapped potential within their employees.[6]

Having human resources (HR) directors with knowledge of workforce trends and the organization is important as they work closely with senior management to develop long-term plans that link HR and organizational goals.[7] The future academic library may require significant involvement from directors of human resources who are familiar with the skills and abilities of current library employees, who have the expertise to design specific training programs and recommend organizational changes after staff leave or retire, and who know which areas of the library organization may require redefining current jobs and hiring professional staff with different skills and expertise to facilitate a long-term, sustainable future.[8]

Four Scenarios

The scenarios used in this study present four possible descriptions of academic research libraries. The scenarios are not mutually exclusive, and they were not intended to be so. Scenario 1 represents current library services and values with a clear focus on traditional collection development. Scenario 2 focuses on discipline-oriented information services, which might include university law school libraries, medical libraries, and even architecture libraries; such libraries are administered by and report to the deans of their respective schools rather than the university librarian. Both Scenarios 1 and 2 are somewhat traditional. Scenario 3 portrays the academic library as a digital repository, knowledge creator, and integrator of information and data. Scenario 4 envisions the academic library as an infrastructure convener. In some cases, the roles of the future university library in Scenarios 3 and 4 may be the responsibility of other campus departments. Some scenarios, such as the infrastructure convener scenario, assign roles to libraries that current members of the academic institutions may not regard as library responsibilities.

Scenario One

DESCRIPTION

The library revolves around the traditional functions of acquiring, housing, organizing, preserving, and making available a wide range of knowledge resources that support the instructional and research missions of the university. Virtual and in-person information services, such as online reference and library research instruction, are emphasized in library instruction sessions in traditional classroom settings. The library includes a number of specialists, with most librarians managing the multiple responsibilities that cut across the traditional functions. Cooperative library collections networks are used extensively to provide backup support and achieve savings in bibliographic control and access to needed materials.

UNIVERSITY CONTEXT

The driving forces include intense economic pressures with across-the-board budget cuts; accountability for effective use of available resources; strong commitment to traditional means of research, teaching, and learning; and a growing readiness to deploy affordable, proven technology. Reducing costs and building fund development capacities are prominent strategies. There are periodic efforts to plan comprehensively and strategically, particularly in light of the changing demographics of students, the new emphasis on the use of electronic information, and changes in the university's curriculum. Scholarly practices, however, are slow to change—limited by lethargy and anxiety among the faculty, particularly in the traditionally strong departments. There are increasing numbers of faculty enthusiastic about the potential of information technology and networking.

PHILOSOPHY AND ROLE

Traditional values characterize the libraries' leadership with an emphasis on services, collections, accountability, costs, and effective management systems. Success of the library system is viewed primarily in terms of growth in collections, relative status among higher education institutions, and reputation for responsiveness to campus interests. The notion of access to information resources is promoted, and there is a deliberate library management strategy of focusing on user needs and striving to satisfy those needs. The library provides newer technologically based services as a supplement to traditional library activities.

Scenario Two

DESCRIPTION

The library repositions itself as a series of sophisticated discipline-oriented information services modeled after the medical field, where national and regional services provide the infrastructure for local agencies to provide timely, user-tailored information support. Such services are available in the humanistic and historical studies, social sciences, physical sciences, and biological sciences and the prominent professional schools through decentralized, institutionalized information units. Public services vary according to the characteristics and needs of the discipline but tend to be personalized and intense, relying extensively on technology for access to required information. The staff consists mainly of subject specialists, with many of the traditional functions of acquiring and cataloging of published literature achieved through commercial and network services. A central library capability exists to operate certain basic instructional support functions, provide document delivery services from the remote storage and central collection, and maintain communication and coordination among local information services and the regional, national, and international agencies relied upon for information access and retrieval.

UNIVERSITY CONTEXT

There is increasing specialization in the research arena, especially big science. In response to growing economic pressures, there is a focus on securing private and federal support to establish cooperative centers that address societal concerns on an interdisciplinary basis. These centers are closely related to the redirection of university organization to emphasize and facilitate the way scholars work together. The use of affinity groups for organizing disciplines has become stronger. Economic pressures have forced a restructuring of the familiar university centralized structure, with budget and program control assigned to the discipline centers. These have become revenue and cost centers with responsibility for fiscal oversight of related activities, including the library.

PHILOSOPHY AND ROLE

The driving forces center on research and teaching practices in the major disciplines and interdisciplinary centers with the library staff following faculty practices most closely and, in effect, serving as silent partners. There is a great deal of diversity in the definition of the university's information services, with success of its services tied to the work of scholars in the discipline or the interdisciplinary centers. As a result, the science information services are measured on the basis of speed, responsiveness, and relevance. The humanistic and historical studies information support is evaluated in terms of breadth, richness, and variety.

Scenario Three

DESCRIPTION

There are fundamental changes to forms of scientific and humanistic communication, and the research library responds by becoming active partners in the knowledge creation process and curators of vast data repositories. In this setting, libraries are exercising creativity and care in what they choose to collect; developing new relationships with research and teaching personnel that are dynamic, visible, and proactive; and working across disciplines and with entire departments. Librarians take on new roles creating new structures for understanding and linking knowledge in ways that scholars can use, organize, and integrate that knowledge; and managing and creating metadata and data "trees" for new knowledge discovery that leads to powerful linking. Librarians are full members of research teams, working at structuring, organizing, and ordering data being generated on large collaborative research initiatives—expanding the conservation role into the generative/creative role. Libraries continue as the intellectual center of campus for student work that is occurring in new formats and new arrangements and for the broader goals of information supply that contribute to faculty productivity and faculty competitiveness in funding arenas. Undergraduate students will be provided comfortable and imaginatively designed study and community space, but Internet information services will increasingly be relied on for instructional support services.

UNIVERSITY CONTEXT

Researchers may work easily in interuniversity research projects irrespective of geographical or organizational location. Students rely on satellite-mediated long-distance communication systems to allow two-way audiovisual and digital conferences, selecting course offerings from a variety of agencies. The university as an organization is quite centralized, coordinating the flow of information to provide the essential services that scholars and students require on a decentralized basis.

PHILOSOPHY AND ROLE

The driving force is the changing nature of knowledge creation and use in a research-intensive institution. The library serves as an active partner in this creative process. Work includes development of knowledge bases (automated encyclopedias), deployment of technology, and system design. Success is determined by the achievement of economies of scale as well as by the provision of sophisticated new information capabilities. With increasing use of personal computers, document delivery, and data banks, the traditional service role is assumed by the end user, with the information center staff serving as brokers among utilities and users.

Scenario Four

DESCRIPTION

The library provides a service-oriented infrastructure through technology that connects users and becomes central to building and sustaining academic communities, which may extend well beyond the home campus. The library plays a convening role for various communities on campus and works closely with the IT unit on campus to develop and implement platforms and tools that facilitate and encourage a culture of participation and collaboration, particularly for the teaching and learning program of the institution. It also develops community (Web 2.0 or Web 3.0) environments for select disciplines, working in cooperation with key faculty and departments. The local integrated library system has disappeared; instead, the library contracts for services, such as circulation, e-reserves, and periodical availability from a large cooperative; such services have moved to the "network level." Institutional users can become part of a conversation about information resources by participating in social networking services developed around information resource collections. More sophisticated, academically oriented recommender systems have been developed, enabling students to benefit from the quality rating given by academics in the field to various online resources.

UNIVERSITY CONTEXT

There is increasing emphasis on using technology to reduce costs and increase revenues by raising enrollments by 40 percent in the next three years without straining the physical resources on campus. Therefore, most students take multiple online courses per semester or one fully online semester in their four-year programs. Academic departments are required to offer a significant percentage of undergraduate courses over the web. Some of these courses are made available through partnerships with other universities, meaning that students receive credit for courses developed and taught by outside faculty. Homework, practice sessions, and laboratory experience are managed entirely through software that frees faculty for teaching, coaching, and research. Some faculty find that holding class and/or office hours in virtual world environments helps to engage fully online students, and the library offers reference and instruction services there as well.

PHILOSOPHY AND ROLE

The phrase "the library is the heart of the campus" develops a new context. The library assures effective seamless access to needed information through an array of services and in an environment incorporating blogs, wikis, portals, and other social networking methods that diminishes the role of librarian as expert and emphasizes the librarian as provider of infrastructure and a designer of information systems. Success is measured by intensity of library involvement in building communities, effectiveness of student and faculty access to and use of information resources, and the integration of information/communication technologies to enable research and learning.

The Case Study Institutions and Choice of Scenarios

At each of the four institutions that were the subjects of the case studies, the library director was asked to choose which scenario among the four could serve as a strategic vision for his or her institution. Two directors (Cases A and D) chose Scenario 3, and two (Cases B and C) chose Scenario 4. No director felt that Scenario 1 or 2 presented strategic futures for today's research libraries. After the director chose a particular scenario and gave it a title, the director of human resources in each of the case study libraries was interviewed to learn what opportunities and challenges the library would face in moving toward the future described in the chosen scenario. The four cases and the scenarios chosen are summarized in table 8.1.

Table 8.1
Summary of Cases and Scenarios Chosen by the Library Directors

Case	University	US Region	Scenario Chosen	Title Chosen
A	publicly funded university	Northeast	3	Research Intensive Model (RIM)
B	publicly funded research university	Southwest	4	Libraries as Infrastructure Providers and Community Builders (LIPCB)
C	publicly funded research university that confers undergraduate, graduate, and professional degrees	Middle Atlantic	4	Proactive Approach (PA)
D	publicly funded research university	Midwest	3	Library as Research Teams (LRT)

The four institutions in this case study are all publicly funded research institutions in the United States that confer undergraduate, graduate, and professional degrees. Case A is located in the northeast United States. The library director chose Scenario 3 and titled it Research Intensive Model (RIM). Case B is a publicly funded research university located in the southwest United States. The library director chose Scenario 4 and titled it Libraries as Infrastructure Providers and Community Builders (LIPCB). Case C, a publicly funded research university, is located in the Middle Atlantic region of the United States and confers undergraduate, graduate, and professional degrees. The library director chose Scenario 4 and titled it Proactive Approach (PA). Case D is a publicly funded research university located in the Midwestern United States. The library director chose Scenario 3 and titled it Library as Research Teams (LRT).

Human Resource Directors in the Four Case Studies

Case A

The director of human resources (DHR) in Case A is not a librarian. She has worked eight years in higher education personnel administration. Before accepting her current position with the libraries, the DHR worked in corporate human resources. The DHR believes RIM closely resembles the library director's vision, but her thoughts on arriving at the scenario are mixed. From her perspective, change is very slow in academia, particularly the steps moving librarians toward becoming active partners in the knowledge creation process or developing new dynamic, visible, proactive relationships with research and teaching personnel; she said both are different from current practice.

Case B

The associate director (AD) in Case B has worked with the library director for more than a decade. His portfolio includes all library collections and services and the in-house human resource operation. His first impression of Scenario 4 was positive. He sees the library as a community builder for campus and believes the institutional repository has contributed to this as faculty store data and digital archives that they want to make available.

Beyond establishing the institutional repository, the library, he notes, wants to become the information hub for a well-developed Web presence. As the library seeks to accomplish Scenario 4, however, researchers should know the content originates from the library. He sees a challenge in providing a convening role on campus if students and researchers access scholarly resources without realizing the role of the library. To address this problem, the library is looking at ways of watermarking some of the databases and digitized resources. According to the AD, library statistics show more patron contact through the website than people reached in a fifty-minute instruction session. He said

> They are coming to our web site in large numbers and this
> has been the biggest mental transition for some of our se-
> nior librarians, in terms of where to spend their time.

Case C

The portfolio for associate university librarian (AUL) in Case C has changed over the years to include all the areas of the library.** The AUL works closely with a personnel librarian who serves as the liaison between the central campus human resource function and the library. The ideas in Scenario 4, said the AUL, resemble future directions for the current organization, but she is not sure the library will settle exactly on the future laid out in the scenario. She said,

> We always think about change, but moving in any future
> direction requires that we take advantage of the opportu-
> nities in the environment.

The AUL believes, that no matter how many ideas there are or how they are communicated, it is hard for people to jump mentally to the future. She said,

> It is difficult to jostle mentally about a future direction
> when librarians tend to take things so literally. But regard-
> less of specifics in scenario 4 or any future scenario, it is
> clear there is going to be a lot more change. So much of how
> we provide library resources has changed. It is amazing to

** The AUL's portfolio includes technical services, collections, public services, budget, planning, human resources, assessment, and technology.

think about what we talked about only 10 years ago so I can only imagine what the future will bring.

Case D

Before accepting the administrative role, the associate director (AD) in Case D served as library faculty with liaison responsibilities. In administration, the AD serves as the link between staff and the library director's vision, a role that clarifies the director's vision with librarians and other staff. Regular communication, the AD believes, helps to advance change even if it is incremental. The AD said

> Every week, I send out a newsletter to communicate our progress. I add in information the library dean wants to share from meetings with the Provost. I just believe it's important to have written communication, [but we also meet] face-to-face [with managers and staff] to share the library… [director's] vision. Since I came up from staff, my credibility helps because they know me, they trust me.

The AD noted that to move to Scenario 4 liaison work, the departments must move beyond communication solely around collections. The AD reminds librarians about the importance of rethinking their skills and abilities, but also recognizes the difficulties involved in redefining existing work.

Responses by the Human Resources Directors

Similarities across All Case Study Sites

All the HR directors recognize the vision in the strategic scenarios. They face similar historical, collective bargaining, and campus human resource practices. Yet they all recognize the opportunity to change the current organization to move toward achieving the strategic vision. Available strategies include strategic hiring, redesign of positions as retirements occur, and assessment of current collection, instruction, and other services to repurpose current positions. While the AD in Case B completely agreed with the directions outlined in Scenario 4, he shared an appreciation for a long-term vision similar to that of his counterparts in Cases A and D. Given their perspectives, these three HR directors (A, B, and D) expressed concern about changes that could occur when the present library director retires and a new director arrives. The long-term personnel changes needed to meet the current director's strategic vision may or may not match the successor director's vision. What remains critical for the future is to make changes that create a new culture.

The DHR in Case A noted that the library's culture is not proactive, but deeply rooted in a traditional university research library, which presents barriers to shifting toward Scenario 3. As with all sites, the AUL in Case C believes that Scenario 4 describes how librarians' traditional roles diminish to make it possible for them to become authorities on new and emerging technologies, the current and emerging platforms for digitization projects, and developments in copyright, open access, and scholarly communication. The AD in Case B said that when communicating with faculty, librarians must move away from traditional questions such as, What books can I order for you? Can I talk to your class about how to use library resources?

The changes, say all the HR directors, will take time. The AD in Case D believes that lasting organizational change may take seven to ten years.

Collectively, the HR directors believe professional development is essential to scale the present organizations toward the chosen strategic vision scenarios. The DHR in Case A questions whether the library can move toward Scenario 3 considering the way that professional development currently occurs in the organization. She asked,

> Are national professional conferences the right venue to train, re-train, or introduce new skills into the organization?

She expressed concerns about the current practice of relying on conference attendance, which, from her perspective, does not encourage or assist librarians in their efforts to learn the skills necessary for Scenario 3 research teams. The AD in Case D agrees and thinks that the library must develop in-house, focused training to help librarians transition from merely assisting end users to, as Scenario 3 suggests, repackaging information and working closely with faculty on research teams.

The HR directors all view hiring the next wave of librarians and other staff as extremely important to moving libraries toward the future. In order to arrive at the strategic scenarios, the HR directors question if the current liaison/subject specialist still works. In Case B, the AD said the library will hire more generalists who know technology. Similarly, in Case C, the AUL said the specialization of the university makes it difficult to change the libraries' support of academic departments, but when the library does not need those specific liaison skills, it hires candidates with the best demonstrated understanding of the technological environment. The AD in Case B reflected

> Especially with retirements, this is an opportunity for those in library administration to ask, does the library need that work done anymore? Are there other priorities that need staff support?

To enact the strategic vision balancing the right mix of librarians and other staff remains a challenge; this is especially true when considering significant change within a union environment.

In the union environments in Cases A and C, the HR directors thought being proactive would be the greater challenge. The DHR in Case A believes the library's culture is not proactive, but the building blocks of any change in library personnel must begin with collective bargaining. While the library directors selected different scenarios from the ones the HR directors preferred, the universities in Cases A, B, and C face similar challenges when dealing with the hiring and job classification policies that come from each campus's central HR department. With campus permission, the AD in Case B designed a stand-alone personnel and evaluation system that more effectively captures the contribution of librarians.

Differences across Case Study Sites

The AD and library director in Case B set aside "strategic opportunity" money. This funding allows individuals at all levels to pursue projects that align with and advance the library's strategic direction. The AD likes this model because as time passes between strategic planning cycles, the strategic opportunity funding process encourages proactive rather than reactive approaches to new ideas and opportunities. Group members who apply for this funding are charged with looking at the bigger picture, which requires talking to deans, department heads, and students rather than just individual faculty. One challenge in moving fully to Scenario 4 is the relationship with campus IT, but the AD, with the agreement of the library director, said

> I can teach librarians technical skills. IT professionals don't have the understanding and approach to access and discovery of information, so just having those technical skills will not do me any good in the future.

At the university in Case A, the library director and provost set aside funding to convert textbooks to open-source platforms to encourage faculty to embrace new models of access. The provost said

> We set aside a very small investment, offering faculty who had a proposal to convert materials that they owned to open source as a replacement to costly textbooks. I think we picked eight faculties and the estimate of savings to the students by posting these open source materials in lieu of purchasing text in the first year was over $70,000 for a $10,000 investment and of course that recurs.

The DHR in Case A believes this partnership model can signal the beginning of redefining librarians' relationships with faculty; however, she thinks Scenario 3 requires additional technical staff and may need librarians to integrate new knowledge like that required to incorporate digitized collections into the teaching curriculum. She believes digitized special collections support Scenario 3, but also require future professional development resources, a more flexible hiring system, and consistent library leadership.

In Case D, the AD believes the director's vision of hiring individuals with PhD degrees in areas other than librarianship represents a flexible approach to establishing a place on the research teams, as Scenario 3 describes. The AD believes improving current hiring practices through the union for the next wave of hiring librarians is critical for the library to realize Scenario 3. The AD said

> I think it has to be all of us moving in a new direction. Certainly we need the systems and technology librarians to lead us toward scenario 3, but of course we need the public user librarians to not just follow, but also lead a little bit too because they are the ones with the contact with the faculty and students. So, it kind of needs to be a coordinated approach.

The gap between current and future services will require more assessment and evaluation. In Case C, the AUL believes

> We will define future directions through our assessment, user studies, and the constant feedback we get from users about what they need. After taking all that in, it is important to remain flexible about changing services.

The AD in Case B also thinks assessment of three areas—information literacy, research services, and digital libraries—supports the new and emerging roles in Scenario 4. Evaluation and assessment, he believes, will become increasingly important in creating the vision in Scenario 4. The assessment team works with strategic planning groups in all three areas and examines the changing technological environment, campus changes, and library organizational development.

The HR directors have different campus policies and procedures to contend with in hiring, collective bargaining, and performance evaluations for the library. In Cases A and B, the central HR office policies pose a challenge to library personnel action. The DHR in Case A said the system is old and outdated, and contended

> The requirements do not reflect the changing nature of jobs, particularly in the library.

While all the HR administrators value hiring toward the strategic vision scenario, several mention the alternatives to professional development. At the university in Case C, the AUL believes training and development are positive for the organization because hiring staff who possess all the new skills and competencies is not a realistic expectation. She knows the organization must support staff and help librarians develop. She likes the design of the professional development at her library, which uses internal people to facilitate training. She said

> Lately, these training sessions focus on improving interactions with the public and how staff might be able to get involved in liaison work. We want to make sure everyone understands what platforms are available, what are the examples of projects with faculty. What do we mean by institutional repository (IR) material? Are there limitations to what we add to the IR? What do we mean by supporting publishing? What are the questions to ask if staff hear about those requests?

The DHR in Case A would approve of this approach, as she questions how university research libraries benefit from current conference attendance that is recognized widely as professional development. The annual review process encourages conference attendance and involvement, but the DHR questions what new perspectives are gained and what actual development of knowledge and skills is provided such attendance that would aid in moving the present organization toward Scenario 3.

Conclusion

All the library directors in the case study agree academic research libraries currently maintain an important, unquestioned place in the academy. Library directors are challenged by unprecedented technological change to articulate that value through a strategic vision. All the library directors recognize how scenarios allow them to communicate the rationale for change, provide a narrative that describes a direction for future services, and articulate to others on campus new roles for librarians. The optimism with which directors create and communicate strategic vision is noteworthy because all the HR directors cited the library's culture as the main barrier to moving the current library toward the future scenario. Thus, these visions of possible futures serve as important internal motivators for changing the culture of the current organization, but they also enable the institution's administration to follow the director's leadership when making decisions about library resources that support the institution.

While the HR directors in the library believe the current organization is far from the scenario selected by their directors, they appreciate a long-term vision and recognize that one deterrent to transformative change within the library might be the nature of the current culture. As members of the senior administrative team, they believe in retraining staff and hiring new employees to expand the traditional research library roles but express concern about the specific, incremental human resource decisions made to move the current organization toward the strategic scenarios. A strategic vision scenario is useful for them as they consider the challenges and barriers to pursuing a strategic vision.

The scenarios incorporate changing external university contexts, technological changes, and institutional cooperation, yet each library director acknowledges that the library will continue to be responsible for its traditional roles in research collection acquisition and access, liaison, and instruction. Through the articulation of a variety of possible futures, the library directors encourage participation by librarians and other staff at all levels in envisioning how future directions of the university research library support their respective institutions.

This study encourages university library directors, directors of human resources, and other members of senior management teams to consider the use of scenarios. As narrative stories, scenarios become a flexible tool that incorporates complexity and uncertainty into the planning process, thereby enabling leaders and staff at all levels of the organization to consider additional factors when planning future directions. There is further value in understanding that leadership is necessary to motivate staff to be capable of achieving the desired future. Lastly, as individuals prepare to assume directorships, they can use scenarios to review and refine their own vision of the future university research library or, more broadly, the future of any college or university library.

Notes

1. Mats Lindgren and Hans Bandhold, *Scenario Planning: The Link between Future and Strategy* (New York: Palgrave MacMillan, 2009).

2. Jon Edward Cawthorne, "Viewing the Future of University Research Libraries through the Perspectives of Scenarios" (PhD diss., Simmons, 2013).

3. David W. Lewis, "A Strategy for Academic Libraries in the First Quarter of the 21st Century," *College and Research Libraries* 68, no. 5 (September 2007): 430.

4. James B. Neal, "Information Anarchy or Information Utopia?" *Chronicle of Higher Education* 52, no. 16 (December 9, 2005): B23, http://chronicle.com/article/Information-Anarchy-or/2773.

5. Pongracz Sennyey, Lyman Ross, and Caroline Mills, "Exploring the Future of Academic Libraries: A Definitional Approach," *Journal of Academic Librarianship* 35, no. 3 (May 2009): 252–59.

6. Denise Stephens and Keith Russell, "Organizational Development, Leadership, Change and the Future of Libraries," *Library Trends* 53, no.1 (2004): 239.

7. Patricia Hawthorne, "Redesigning Library Human Resources: Integrating Human Resources Management and Organizational Development," *Library Trends* 53, no.1 (2004): 172–173.

8. Ibid., 175

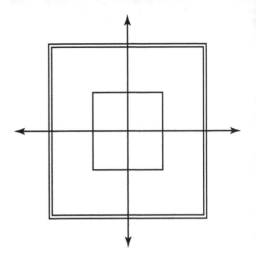

CHAPTER 9

UNIVERSITY OF NEBRASKA– LINCOLN STUDENT TECHNOLOGY FEE CASE STUDY UPDATED

Joan Giesecke and Deb Pearson

IN 1996, THE University of Nebraska–Lincoln (UNL) used scenario planning to determine how to establish and use a student technology fee to provide ongoing computer support for students through the office of the vice chancellor for information services (IS). The outcome of the planning process was a list of agreed-to uses for the student technology fee that was approved by the administration and by the student government. The list set the direction for how services to students would be provided and updated as technology and student needs changed. The scenario planning process was so successful at outlining plausible futures that the list of uses for the technology fee is still used today with few modifications.

The case study of the UNL scenario planning process was included in the book *Scenario Planning for Libraries*, published in 1998. The case study is reproduced in part in this chapter with an update on how Information Technology Services (ITS) has modified the use of the student technology fee to address unanticipated changes in technology.[1]

Student Technology Fee: A Case Study at the University of Nebraska–Lincoln

Background

As was true at most universities, UNL faced the problem of increasing demand for computer support services by students in a time of decreasing support from the state for the university. By 1996 the support crisis was becoming critical and the associate vice chancellor for information services determined that something different had to be done if the computing area was to provide even basic services to students. The idea of charging a student fee was proposed internally within IS and was discussed as one way to obtain ongoing funding. The IS computing managers met in the summer of 1996 to brainstorm how a student fee might be used. The list of services generated by this internal group was very basic and concentrated on upgrading current hardware and software.

In June 1996 the associate vice chancellor for information services concluded that the group needed to have a more imaginative, innovative proposal if it were to capture the imagination of the chancellor, vice chancellors, deans, faculty, and students. The proposal had to appeal to and have the support of the students to be accepted by the administration and by the board of regents.

The associate vice chancellor for IS suggested scenario planning as the tool to use to help the managers move beyond their own views of reality and of the future to develop a more forward-thinking proposal. It was felt that scenario planning would help the group explore a wide range of possible futures to aid the UNL leadership's decision-making process.

Process

A scenario planning team of fifteen persons was assembled. The majority of team membership came from within the department of Information Services, a large educational support unit that includes libraries, telecommunications, and computer services. Student representatives were from the senate computational services committee and university library student employee pool. The chair of the Faculty Teaching and Learning Technology Roundtable contributed a teaching perspective to the team.

It is important to note here that the planning team represented the key groups that would be affected by a student technology fee and included representatives that were most likely to be directly involved in the services that a fee would support. By involving in the planning process those closest to the problems of student access to technology, the managers felt they would benefit from a fresh perspective on the issue and could begin to identify problems that would arise in trying to implement yet another fee for students. The planning group was provided with reading materials on the use of scenario planning, provided examples from the literatures of successful teamwork tasks in this area, and given the opportunity to develop a supportable list of benefits resulting from a student technology fee at UNL.

Given the narrow focus of the problem facing the planning team, the team chose to follow David Mercer's simpler process for developing mini-scenarios rather than using a full scenario planning process (see chapter 2). Mercer uses six steps to create a more focused scenario planning process:

- identifying drivers for change
- linking the key factors
- producing the initial mini-scenarios
- reducing the number of scenarios
- writing the scenarios
- identifying issues that arise[2]

Identifying the Drivers for Change

Two meetings of the team were planned. Much of the first meeting was dedicated to the process—learning about scenario planning, reviewing the team charge, and listening to assumptions on the subject at hand. This session concluded with a period of unrestricted brainstorming on the environment for technology and on the factors that were likely to have an impact on student use of technology on campus. A faculty colleague, experienced with the scenario planning process, opened the meeting with an overview of his experiences and provided valuable assurance that positive results were possible from this investment in energies and resources.

The group then broke into two subgroups to identify factors in the environment that would have an impact on student use of technology. These brainstorming sessions resulted in two extensive lists of more than thirty elements. The elements ranged from the mundane, such as a need for an easier way to obtain a parking permit, to the more controversial, such as how to upgrade faculty skills to meet growing student expectations about the use of technology. The planning group then adjourned for one week to give the team leaders an opportunity to consolidate the information from the first session and to provide participants with feedback for the second session.

Linking the Key Factors

In the week between the two planning sessions, the four managers who served as team leaders met to codify the notes from the brainstorming sessions and to set the stage for the first attempts at scenario criterion. They consolidated and reviewed the brainstorming lists. This smaller group used the lists to identify two factors considered most important and most uncertain: the skill level of students entering the university and the types of services students would want to support. The consensus of the steering committee was that these two factors provided a broad enough framework to consider the issues under discussion.

The factors were listed on a continuum to form the matrix for scenario development. Skill level was measured from low-skill students with little or no experience with or exposure to computers to high-skill students who own their own computers. Student having low technological skill do not generally rely on it and are uncertain about its value. Students having high technological skill are very dependent on it, demanding to use it at all times and in all places possible. Services were described on a continuum from innovative cutting-edge services and technology to production-oriented, basic services. Innovative activities would be experimental activities based on emerging, bleeding-edge technologies, such as a metropolitan area wireless data network. Production services would be reliable services based on current, proven technologies, such as the current Ethernet networks. The matrix from these two factors described the possible scenario stories: high-skill students interested in cutting-edge services; high-skill students interested in production services; low-skill students curious about cutting-edge technology; and low-skill students seeking basic, efficient services.

Although usually the whole planning group would be involved in choosing the factors that frame the scenario development, the team leaders decided that in the interests of time they would complete this step themselves. However, the team leaders were careful to be sure that the major issues identified by participants were covered in the matrix design.

Producing the Initial Mini-scenario Elements

The second planning session, held one week later, started with a brief recap of session one and a description of the matrix and the four possible scenarios. The group then divided into two subgroups to generate the key elements they believed should be a part of each of the four possible scenarios. The groups came back together to share these lists and decide on the common elements to be included in each scenario.

Reducing the Number of Scenarios to Two

The team leaders met again after the planning session to consolidate the input and to look for common elements that would allow the team to develop two of the scenarios into stories to be shared in the planning process. The group chose to divide the scenarios based on student skill level, outlining a scenario for low-skill students and one for high-skill students. The team leaders wanted to be sure that the scenarios focused on student needs and not on technology so that the students would able to see what benefits they might get from a student technology fee.

Writing the Scenarios

One member of the team then volunteered to draft an initial story for each of the scenarios, incorporating the elements outlined by the planning group. The stories were written from the student viewpoint, focusing on how a student might use technology on campus once the fee was in place and new equipment and services were available. Each story started with two new students beginning classes in the fall semester and discussed how the students would encounter and use technology in their first few weeks at the university. The low-skill students were described as inexperienced but curious about technology, a bit afraid of using the various computer services, and in need of supportive training programs. The high-skill students were viewed as having high expectations of the type of technology they would find on campus and as wanting to immediately plug into the technology system. Using the simpler scenario planning process, only two scenarios were developed to describe the students' skill levels.

The draft stories were shared among the team leaders, edited, and polished for sharing with the planning group. (The completed scenarios are included in the case study in *Scenario Planning for Libraries*.)[3]

Identifying Issues That Arise

The final step in the scenario process was to develop strategies that would be most likely to succeed if either of the scenarios proved to be an apt description of the student expectations for technology. The group created a recommended list of possible expenditures that could be made with the technology funds. To determine what could actually then be done, the team leaders took the list of possible items or activities to fund with a technology fee as developed in the various planning group sessions and mapped the list to the four quadrants of the matrix. Those items that fit three or four of the quadrants were then examined to see if they appeared to be good purchases from the technology fee. For example, increasing student access to computers and upgrading computer equipment in the public labs was seen as benefiting students with low skills needing both production services and some innovative technology and high-skill students seeking production services. High-skill students seeking advanced, cutting-edge equipment would need a more specialized lab area. Creating a student-centered leaning space by placing a computer lab in the libraries and incorporating it into the regular electronic library services was also seen as benefiting most of the student groups. Adding a text and technology area to the library lab would make the space more useful to high-skill, innovative students.

The Case Study Revisited

For the past fifteen years, UNL computing services, working with the student government, has used the same two scenarios and the list of possible uses of the technology fee to determine how to best use the student fee. The driving forces of student skill level and type of service desired have been particularly helpful, although the definition of student skill level has evolved. Low-skill students today are those students who believe they are proficient in their use of technology and are comfortable with social media and gaming software. However, they are less proficient with creating documents, using multimedia in their coursework, and using specialized software. They are also reluctant to ask for help because they do not believe they need to learn to use software. Rather, they think they can simply turn on the software and it will work. High-skill students are still using cutting-edge software and hardware and need access to specialized labs for the products they are unlikely to purchase for themselves. The type of services desired by students can still be described on a continuum from production-level services, which now include access to multimedia services, to innovative services including access to 3-D printers and other high-end equipment.

Funding continuing improvements in the network has been a key use of the student fee. While initially it was believed that network improvement would come from expanding access to the Ethernet network, today it is clear that enhancing Wi-Fi access is most important to the students. Because the planning process looked at plausible, multiple futures, the computing services and network units continued to look at options rather than thinking in terms of one preferred future. As a result, they moved to wireless network options as soon as use began to grow in this area rather than remaining focused solely on wired connections. By thinking in terms of options and multiple solutions, they were prepared to expand the wireless network and were able to accommodate mobile technology, smartphones, and students bringing multiple devices to campus without having to redo the planning process.

Not all ideas from the initial list of funding options proved to be needed. Some items, such as providing opportunities for students to teach in the classroom, were not seen as important by students. Although students may teach and do presentations, their technology needs mirror those of the faculty and are supported by campus upgrades to classrooms. Student fees are not used for general classroom upgrades. Providing internships to work with faculty on technology use was also not funded as there was little demand from faculty or students for this service. Table 9.1 summarizes the initial ideas that were proposed for the technology fee and identifies those that have been supported by the fee. In all, half of the initial ideas have been supported. Those items that were not funded through the technology fee were either funded from other sources or were not supported by the students. Interestingly, no new items were added to the list. Rather the students found that the list provided enough flexibility to give them the services they most wanted to support through student fees.

Lessons Learned

The scenario planning process proved to be an extremely effective planning tool for UNL. The process helped the computing managers think beyond their own experiences. They found that thinking in terms of plausible futures rather than one preferred future gave them more flexibility

Table 9.1
Uses for the UNL Technology Fee

Strategy from 1997	Production or Innovative Strategy	Items Funded through 2013
Develop student peer mentoring.	Production/ Innovation	Part of computer lab and help desk services.
Improve network.	Production/ Innovation	Funds moved from wired to wireless network expansion.
Increase student access to equipment and student labs.	Production/ Innovation	Upgrade equipment every 3–4 years. Added laptop checkout services.
Provide opportunity for students to teach in classroom.	Production	Not funded.
Support faculty development.	Production/ Innovation	Training for faculty in using technology in the classroom.
Create multimedia center for students.	Innovative	Upgrades of two multimedia labs continue.
Survey/visit peer institutions.	Production	Travel is not funded from student fees.
Create student-centered learning space and environment in libraries.	Production/ Innovation	Continue to upgrade library learning commons.
Provide greater access to existing electronic resources.	Production	Fees help offset inflationary increases for electronic resources.
Provide more electronic resources.	Production	Supports new resources as student needs change.
Develop easy interfaces.	Innovation	Improve learning management system; add building blocks to Blackboard.
Create Internet courses.	Innovation	Distance education courses are funded through tuition and other fees.
Provide access to experts.	Innovation	Computer help center.
Provide internships with faculty.	Innovation	Not funded, not supported by students.
Increase data storage.	Innovation	Not funded from fees.
Promote technology literacy.	Production/ Innovation	Evolved from classes to online tutorials.

Table 9.1
Uses for the UNL Technology Fee

Disseminate information about services.	Production	Funded from state funds.
Integrate technology into university business functions.	Production	Limited activity related to student fees.
Develop strategic flexibility.	Innovation	Planning remains flexible based on scenarios.
Upgrade supported classrooms.	Production	Funded by university.
Provide multimedia classroom orientation.	Production	Service not desired by students.

in responding to the changing environment of technology. The use of a broad-based planning committee brought a variety of perspectives into the process and helped ensure that the scenarios were robust enough to address present and future needs. The driving forces gave the managers a way to explain the scenarios to each new student fee committee. The creation of the four funding categories—access to technology, support for use of technology, sensitivity to different user skills, and network infrastructure—provided overall guidance for ITS in reviewing annual plans for the student technology fee. The detailed list of possible services provided the students with a guide for the ways that their fees could most effectively be used to support their computing needs.

Perhaps most significantly, using a scenario planning process has helped computing services defend the use of the fee to administrators. As new administrators were hired and new students joined the student government fee committee, ITS managers have explained how the scenario planning process was used. They find that the institution-developed scenarios still resonate with the campus, more so than scenarios that might be developed elsewhere. The inclusion of the many stakeholder groups and the identification of driving forces that related to the values and concerns of the campus have been particularly helpful. These demonstrate how institution-specific processes can be more effective than using scenarios developed elsewhere, which may not reflect the culture of the institution. One measure of success of the process is that, despite budget challenges for the campus, the student technology fee continues to be used to support core needs of students and has not been diverted to other areas that need financial resources.

Conclusion

One lesson that is clear from this process is that planning for a changing environment requires that decision makers think in terms of long-range possibilities as well as near-term needs. Scenario planning, by exploring multiple paths to the future, provides the flexibility that is needed for organizations to adapt and respond to change. Developing scenarios that match the values and culture of the organization and using those stories to help decision makers in their planning efforts can be very effective in addressing the need to remain flexible in times of change.

Notes

1. Joan Giesecke, *Scenario Planning for Libraries* (Chicago: American Library Association, 1998): 80–86.
2. David Mercer, "Simpler Scenarios," *Management Decisions* 33, no. 4 (July 1995): 33.
3. Giesecke, *Scenario Planning for Libraries*, 91–94.

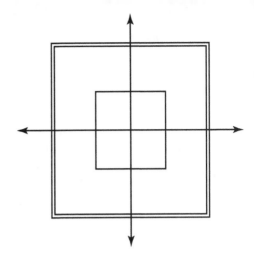

BIBLIOGRAPHY

Abd El Ghaffar, Ahmed, Katrin Alberding, Vasily Nicholsky, and Anaken Lai. *Scenario Thinking: Vision 2020.* St. Andrews, UK: St. Andrews University Press, 2005.

Alvesson, Mats, and Stegan Sveningsson. *Changing Organizational Culture: Cultural Change Work in Progress.* New York: Routledge, 2008.

Association of Research Libraries and Stratus, Inc. *The ARL 2030 Scenarios: A User's Guide for Research Libraries.* Washington, DC: Association of Research Libraries, October 2010.

Babbie, Earl R. *The Practice of Social Research*, 13th ed. Belmont, CA: Wadsworth Cengage Learning, 2012.

Beck, Susan, and Kate Manuel. *Practical Research Methods for Librarians and Information Professionals.* New York: Neal-Schuman, 2008.

Caldwell, Roger. "Two Scenarios for the University of Arizona in 2025." University of Arizona, January 28, 2009. http://cals.arizona.edu/dean/planning/rlc-ua-scenarios-jan09.pdf.

Cameron, Kim. "A Process for Changing Organizational Culture." In *Handbook of Organizational Development,* edited by Thomas G. Cummings, 429–45. Thousand Oaks, CA: Sage, 2008.

Carpenter, Marie, Jolie Graybill, Jerome Offord Jr., and Mary Piorun. "Envisioning the Library's Role in Scholarly Communication in the Year 2025." *portal: Libraries and the Academy* 11, no. 2 (April 2011): 659–81. doi:10.1353/pla.2011.0014.

Cascio, Jamais. "Futures Thinking: Writing Scenarios." *Fast Company,* February 24, 2010. www.fastcompany.com/1560416/futures-thinking-writing-scenarios.

Cawthorne, Jon Edward. "Viewing the Future of University Research Libraries through the Perspectives of Scenarios." PhD diss., Simmons, 2013.

Chadwick, Cynthia, Renee DiPilato, Monique le Conge, Rachel Rubin, and Gary Shaffer. "The Future of the FDLP in Public Libraries." *Public Libraries* 51, no. 4 (July/August 2012): 40–47.

Chermack, Thomas J. "Improving Decision-Making with Scenario Planning." *Futures* 36, no. 3 (April 2004): 295–306. doi:10.1016/S0016-3287(03)00156-3.

———. "A Methodology for Assessing Performance-Based Scenario Planning." *Journal of Leadership and Organizational Studies*, 10, no. 2 (Fall 2003): 55–63. doi:10.1177/107179190301000206.

———. *Scenario Planning in Organizations: How to Create, Use, and Access Scenarios.* San Francisco: Berrett-Koehler, 2011.

Crumpton, Michael A. "Strategic Positioning for Staff Realignment." *Bottom Line* 25, no. 4 (2012): 143–48.

Curtis, Geoff, Claire Davies, Max Hammond, Rob Hawtin, Gill Ringland, and Chris Yapp. *Academic Libraries of the Future: Scenarios beyond 2020.* Academic Libraries of the Future Project, 2011. Reports available: http://www.foresightfordevelopment.org/sobipro/download-file/46-79/54

Enders, Jürgen, Jon File, Jeroen Huisman, and Don Westerheijden, eds. *The European Higher Education and Research Landscape 2020: Scenarios and Strategic Debates.* University of Twente, The Netherlands: Center for Higher Education Policy Studies, 2005. www.utwente.nl/bms/cheps/publications/Publications%202005/Enders05european.pdf.

Fortado, Bruce, and Paul Fadil. "The Four Faces of Organizational Culture." *Competitiveness Review* 22, no. 4 (2012): 283–98.

Giesecke, Joan. *Scenario Planning for Libraries.* Chicago: American Library Association, 1998.

Haegeman, Karel. *The Future State of Higher Education in Europe: Mini-scenarios for 2025.* Seville, Spain: European Commission, January 25, 2011. www.edu2025.ro/UserFiles/File/IPTS.pdf.

Hawthorne, Patricia. "Redesigning Library Human Resources: Integrating Human Resources Management and Organizational Development." *Library Trends* 53, no.1 (2004): 172–86.

Heracleous, Loizos, and Claus D. Jacobs. "Developing Strategy: The Serious Business of Play." In *Business Leadership: A Jossey-Bass Reader*, 2nd ed., edited by Joan Gallos, 324–35. San Francisco: Jossey-Bass, 2008.

Hernon, Peter. *Shaping the Future: Advancing the Understanding of Leadership.* Santa Barbara, CA: Libraries Unlimited, 2010.

Hernon, Peter, and Laura Saunders. "The Federal Depository Library Program in 2023: One Perspective on the Transition to the Future." *College and Research Libraries* 70, no.4 (2009): 351–70.

Huisman, Jeroen, Harry de Boer, and Paulo Charles Pimental Botas. "The Future of English Higher Education: The Changing Landscape." Unpublished manuscript. www.utwente.nl/mb/cheps/publications/Publications%20 2011/LFHE%20Changing%20landscape%20paper%20final%20edit%20 JH.pdf.

Jantz, Ronald C. "A Framework for Studying Organizational Innovation in Research Libraries." *College and Research Libraries* 73, no. 6 (November 2012): 525–41. doi:10.5860/crl-302.

Keough, Shawn M., and Kevin J. Shanahan. "Scenario Planning: Toward a More Complete Model for Practice." *Advances in Developing Human Resources* 10, no. 2 (May 2008): 166–78. doi:10.1177/1523422307313311.

Landeta, Jon. "Current Validity of the Delphi Method in Social Sciences." *Technological Forecasting and Social Change* 73, no. 5 (June 2006): 467–82. doi:10.1016/j.techfore.2005.09.002.

Lewis, David W. "A Strategy for Academic Libraries in the First Quarter of the 21st Century." *College and Research Libraries* 68, no. 5 (September 2007): 418–34. doi:10.5860/crl.68.5.418.

Lindgren, Mats, and Hans Bandhold. *Scenario Planning: The Link between Future and Strategy.* New York: Palgrave Macmillan, 2009.

Linstone, Harold, and Murray Turoff. *The Delphi Method: Techniques and Applications.* Reading, PA: Addison-Wesley, 1975.

Losey, Michael R., Sue Meisinger, and David Ulrich, eds. *The Future of Human Resources Management: Sixty-Four Thought Leaders Explore the Critical HR Issues of Today and Tomorrow.* Alexandria, VA: Society for Human Resource Management, 2005.

Ludwig, Deborah and Jennifer Church-Duran, "Scenario Planning: Developing a Strategic Agenda for Organizational Alignment," *Research Library Issues,* no. 278 (March 2012): 8, http://publications.arl.org/rli278.

Ludwig, Logan, Joan Giesecke, and Linda Walton. "Scenario Planning: A Tool for Academic Health Sciences Libraries." *Health Information and Libraries Journal* 27, no. 1 (March 2010): 28–36.

Martin, Joanne. *Cultures in Organizations: Three Perspectives.* New York: Oxford University Press, 1992.

Martin, Joanne, Martha S. Feldman, Mary Jo Hatch, and Sim B. Sitkin. "The Uniqueness Paradox in Organizational Stories." *Administrative Science Quarterly* 28 (1983): 438–52.

Martino, Joseph P. "The Precision of Delphi Estimates." *Technological Forecasting* 1, no. 3 (March 1970): 293–99. doi:10.1016/0099-3964(70)90030-X.

Mercer, David. "Simpler Scenarios." *Management Decision* 33, no. 4 (July 1995): 32–40. 10.1108/00251749510084662.

Mietzner, Dana, and Guido Reger. "Advantages and Disadvantages of Scenario Approaches for Strategic Foresight." *International Journal of Technology Intelligence and Planning* 1, no. 2 (2005): 220–239.

Neal, James B. "Information Anarchy or Information Utopia?" *Chronicle of Higher Education* 52, no. 16 (December 9, 2005): B23. http://chronicle.com/article/Information-Anarchy-or/2773.

Organisation for Economic Co-operation and Development. "Four Future Scenarios for Higher Education." Paper, OECD/France International Conference, Higher Education to 2030, Paris, France, December 8–9, 2008. www.oecd.org/education/skills-beyond-school/42241931.pdf.

———. *Higher Education to 2030, Volume 2: Globalisation.* Paris: OECD Publishing, 2009. www.mfdps.si/Files//Knjiznica/higher%20educational%202030%20OECD.pdf.

———. "Six Scenarios for Universities." Discussion paper, OECD/CERI Experts Meeting on "University Futures and New Technologies," Washington, DC, January 12, 2005. Excerpted from Stéphan Vincent-Lancrin, "Building Futures Scenarios for Universities and Higher Education: An International Approach," *Policy Futures in Education* 2, no. 2 (2004): 245–62. www.oecd.org/edu/skills-beyond-school/36758932.pdf.

Parente, Frederick J., Janet K. Anderson, Patrick Myers, and Thomas O'Brien. "An Examination of Factors Contributing to Delphi Accuracy." *Journal of Forecasting* 3, no. 2 (April/June1984): 173–82. doi:10.1002/for.3980030205.

Ralston, Bill, and Ian Wilson. *The Scenario Planning Handbook: A Practitioner's Guide to Developing and Using Scenarios to Direct Strategy in Today's Uncertain Times.* Mason, OH: Thomson Higher Education, 2006.

Ringland, Gill. *Scenario Planning: Managing for the Future*, 2nd ed. Winchester, NY: Wiley and Sons, 2006.

Rowe, Gene, George Wright, and Andy McColl. "Judgment Change during Delphi-like Procedures: The Role of Majority Influence, Expertise, and Confidence." *Technological Forecasting and Social Change* 72, no. 4 (May 2005): 377–99. doi:10.1016/j.techfore.2004.03.004.

Schein, Edgar. *Organizational Culture and Leadership*, 3rd ed. San Francisco: Jossey-Bass, 2004.

Schoemaker, Paul J. H. "Scenario Planning: A Tool for Strategic Thinking." *MIT Sloan Management Review* 36, no. 2 (Winter 1995): 25–40.

Schwartz, Peter. *The Art of the Long View: Planning for the Future in an Uncertain World.* New York: Doubleday, 1991.

Senge, Peter. *The Fifth Discipline: The Art and Practice of the Learning Organization.* New York: Doubleday, 1990.

Sennyey, Pongracz, Lyman Ross, and Caroline Mills. "Exploring the Future of Academic Libraries: A Definitional Approach." *Journal of Academic Librarianship* 35, no. 3 (May 2009): 252–59.

Shepston, Carol, and Lyn Curries. "Transforming the Academic Library: Creating an Organizational Culture That Fosters Staff Success." *Journal of Academic Librarianship* 34, no. 4 (July 2008): 358–68.

Simpson, Daniel G. "Key Lessons for Adopting Scenario Planning in Diversified Company," *Planning Review* 20, no. 3 (May/June 1992): 10–48. doi:10.1108/eb054355.

Southern African Regional Universities Association. *Building Higher Education Scenarios 2025: A Strategic Agenda for Development in SADC.* SARUA Leadership Dialogue Series, vol. 3, no. 2. Johannesburg, South Africa: SARUA, 2012. www.sarua.org/files/publications/SARUA%20leadership%20Dialogue%20Series/Leadership%20Dialogue%20Series%20Vol%203%20No%202.pdf.

Staley, David J. *Futures Thinking for Academic Librarians: Scenarios for the Future of the Book.* Chicago: Association of College and Research Libraries, May 2012.

Staley, David J., and Kara J. Malenfant. *Futures Thinking for Academic Librarians: Higher Education in 2025.* Chicago: Association of College and Research Libraries, June 2010.

Stephens, Denise, and Keith Russell. "Organizational Development, Leadership, Change and the Future of Libraries." *Library Trends* 53, no.1 (2004): 238–57.

Sun, Shili. "Organizational Culture and Its Themes." *International Journal of Business and Management* 3, no. 12 (2008): 137–41.

Swanson, Richard A. "Seeing Scenarios." *Advances in Developing Human Resources* 10, no. 2 (May 2008): 127–28. doi:10.1177/1523422307313335.

Universiti Sains Malaysia, comp. *Constructing Future Higher Education Scenarios: Insights from Universiti Sains Malaysia.* Pulau Pinang: Universiti Sains Malaysia, 2007. http://globalhighered.files.wordpress.com/2010/08/con_future.pdf.

University of California. *UC 2025: The Power and Promise of Ten.* Sacramento: University of California, 2006. www.universityofcalifornia.edu/future/lrgt1106.pdf (page now discontinued).

US General Accounting Office. *Case Study Evaluations.* Washington, DC: General Accounting Office, 1990.

van der Merwe, Louis. "Scenario-Based Strategy in Practice: A Framework." *Advances in Developing Human Resources* 10, no. 2 (May 2008): 216–39. doi:10.1177/1523422307313321.

Vignesh, S. N. "The Future Scenario of Digital Library Era." *SRELS Journal of Information Management* 46, no. 1 (March 2009): 25–28.

Wade, Woody. *Scenario Planning: A Field Guide to the Future.* Hoboken, NJ: John Wiley and Sons, 2012.

Walters, Tyler. "The Future of Knowledge Creation and Production in University Research Programs and Their Effect on University Libraries." PhD diss., Simmons, 2013.

———. "The Future Role of Publishing Services in University Libraries." *portal: Libraries and the Academy* 12, no. 4 (October 2012): 425–54. doi:10.1353/pla.2012.0041.

Wildemuth, Barbara. *Applications of Social Research Methods to Questions in Information and Library Science.* Westport, CT: Libraries Unlimited, 2009.

Yin, Robert K. *Case Study Research: Design and Methods.* Los Angeles: Sage, 2014.